The California Gold Rush an   ...usn. The History of America's Most Famous Gold Rushes

By Charles River Editors

Advertisement for sailing to San Francisco amidst the Gold Rush

About Charles River Editors

Charles River Editors provides superior editing and original writing services across the digital publishing industry, with the expertise to create digital content for publishers across a vast range of subject matter. In addition to providing original digital content for third party publishers, we also republish civilization's greatest literary works, bringing them to new generations of readers via ebooks.

Sign up here to receive updates about free books as we publish them, and visit Our Kindle Author Page to browse today's free promotions and our most recently published Kindle titles.

Introduction

Illustration in Harpers Ferry of a "49er" panning gold

The California Gold Rush

"As the spring and summer of 1848 advanced, the reports came faster and faster from the gold-mines at Sutter's saw-mill. Stories reached us of fabulous discoveries, and spread throughout the land. Everybody was talking of "Gold! gold!!" until it assumed the character of a fever. Some of our soldiers began to desert; citizens were fitting out trains of wagons and pack-mules to go to the mines. We heard of men earning fifty, five hundred, and thousands of dollars per day..." – William Tecumseh Sherman

One of the most important and memorable events of the United States' westward push across the frontier came with the discovery of gold in the lands that became California in January 1848. Located thousands of miles away from the country's power centers on the east coast at the time, the announcement came a month before the Mexican-American War had ended, and among the very few Americans that were near the region at the time, many of them were Army soldiers who were participating in the war and garrisoned there. San Francisco was still best known for being a Spanish military and missionary outpost during the colonial era, and only a few hundred called it home. Mexico's independence, and its possession of those lands, had come only a generation earlier.

Everything changed almost literally overnight. While the Mexican-American War technically concluded with a treaty in February 1848, the announcement brought an influx of an estimated 90,000 "Forty-Niners" to the region in 1849, hailing from other parts of America and even as far away as Asia. All told, an estimated 300,000 people would come to California over the next few years, as men dangerously trekked thousands of miles in hopes of making a fortune, and in a span of months, San Francisco's population exploded, making it one of the first mining boomtowns to truly spring up in the West. This was a pattern that would repeat itself across the West anytime a mineral discovery was made, from the Southwest and Tombstone to the Dakotas and Deadwood. Of course, that was made possible by the collective memory of the original California gold rush.

Despite the mythology and the romantic portrayals that helped make the California Gold Rush, most of the individuals who came to make a fortune struck out instead. The gold rush was a boon to business interests, which ensured important infrastructure developments like the railroad and the construction of westward paths, but ultimately, it also meant that big business reaped most of the profits associated with mining the gold. While the Forty-Niners are often remembered for panning gold out of mountain streams, it required advanced mining technology for most to make a fortune.

Nevertheless, the California Gold Rush became an emblem of the American Dream, and the notion that Americans could obtain untold fortunes regardless of their previous social status. As historian H.W. Brands said of the impact the gold rush had on Americans at the time, "The old American Dream ... was the dream of the Puritans, of Benjamin Franklin's 'Poor Richard'... of men and women content to accumulate their modest fortunes a little at a time, year by year by year. The new dream was the dream of instant wealth, won in a twinkling by audacity and good luck… [it] became a prominent part of the American psyche only after Sutter's Mill." While the gold rush may not have made every Forty-Niner rich, the events still continue to influence the country's collective mentality.

This book comprehensively covers the history and legacy of the gold rush that took place from 1848-1855, analyzing how it affected the participants and the nation at large. Along with pictures and a bibliography, you will learn about the California Gold Rush like you never have before, in no time at all.

Picture of a miner on White Pass Trail

The Klondike Gold Rush

"Alaska is the land of the Nineteenth Century Argonauts; and the Golden Fleece hidden away among its snowcapped and glacier-clad mountains is not the pretty creation of mythological fame, but yellow nuggets which may be transformed into the coin of the realm. The vast territory into which these hardy soldiers of fortune penetrate is no less replete with wonders than the fabled land into which Jason is said to have led his band of adventurers. There is this difference, however, between the frozen land of the North and the fabled land of mythology. There is nothing conjectural about Alaska or its golden treasure. Jason led his band into an unknown country without the certain knowledge that the treasure he was seeking was there." – A.C. Harris, author of *Alaska and the Klondike Gold Mines* (1897)

When gold was discovered in the Yukon and Alaska almost 50 years after the rush in California, it drew tens of thousands of prospectors despite the unforgiving climate. Mineral resources had gone a long way in the United States acquiring Alaska a generation earlier, but the lack of transportation kept all but the most dedicated from venturing into the Yukon and Alaska until the announcement of the gold rush. For a few years, the attention turned to the Northwest, and thanks to vivid descriptions by writers like Jack London, the nation became intrigued with the idea of miners toughing out the winter conditions to find hidden gold. Of course, despite the mythology and the romantic portrayals that helped make the Klondike Gold Rush, most of the individuals who came to make a fortune struck out instead.

This book tells the story of the last great gold rush in North America. Along with pictures and a bibliography, you will learn about the Klondike Gold Rush like you never have before, in no time at all.

The California Gold Rush

Chapter 1: The Source of California's Gold

400 million years ago, California existed as a chain of offshore islands and a seafloor dominated by underwater hot springs. While the ash and lavas slowly built up the land area of California itself, the deposits of sulfides proved the most important resource for California's future: gold. The next 200 million years witnessed a period of titanic crustal collisions, as the offshore islands were crushed and folded, along with the volcanic rocks. This metamorphic process created a significant layer of bedrock of the gold areas of future California, known as the Mother Lode region, and the end of the 200 million period resulted in the tectonic forces of the planet pushing the Californian sea floor underneath the North American continent.

The materials did not rest in the subduction zone but rose to the surface of the crust, melted into magma by the interior heat of the planet. The materials then came to the surface through the power of volcanic eruptions, and as the lava cooled slowly, it formed the granitic rock of a giant mountain range, the Sierra Nevadas.[1] From there, water and heat served as the main agents of the dispersal of gold into the Sierra Nevadas. Rain and melted snow percolated into the ground and came into contact with hot molten magma, dissolving the mineral resources, which consisted not only of gold but also other precious m metals like quartz, silver, copper, and zinc. A stew was produced of metals and sulfides and rose to the surface through the fractures in the crust. The stew finally dried as quartz veins in the rocks or came to the surface in the process of hydrothermal mineralization.

When the forces of erosion stripped these layers of rock, they exposed the veins of gold to the elements and began to carry gold particles down the sides of mountains. Some gold was deposited in stream beds, other particles were left as patches of gold on the sides of mountains or valley plateaus, and other gold was covered up by lava flows and layers of sediment.[2]

---

[1] Garry Hayes, "Mining History and Geology of the California Gold Rush," http://hayesg.faculty.mjc.edu/Gold_Rush.html;

[2] Garry Hayes, "Mining History and Geology of the California Gold Rush," http://hayesg.faculty.mjc.edu/Gold_Rush.html;

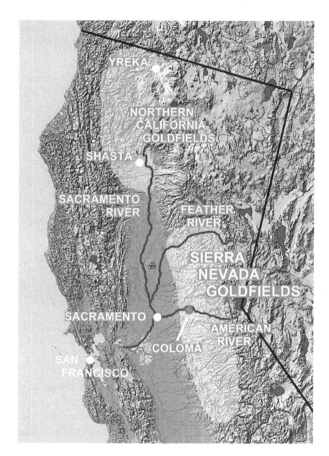

The main goldfields in California

The most important thing was the location of the gold, as most of it lay on the surface of the ground. It belonged to no one except the people who were willing to accomplish the tough work of mining the element.

Chapter 2: The Discovery of Gold

SUTTER'S MILL AT COLOMA
A reproduction of photograph in possession of Charles B. Turrill, of San Francisco, from original daguerreotype taken on the spot by R. H. Vance in 1850. James W. Marshall in the foreground.

1850 picture of Sutter's Mill

The discovery of California's abundant gold was made in such an inauspicious manner that it was almost too amazing to be believed. While Mexicans from the state of Sonora immigrated to California for the purpose of mining, the American adventurers before 1848 had come for a climate and soil conducive for agriculture. Mexico had long meant to find colonists for the region, and Americans, along with Britons, made acceptable applicants. The new landowners saw plenty of room to dominate the region, given the ease to hold large land grants; and many thought of themselves as "new" Californio land barons.

John Sutter belonged to this generation of rare men that settled California with dreams of amassing a huge plot of land. Sutter was a Mexican citizen who had been born in Germany, and near New Helvetia (present-day Sacramento), he planned to sell lumber for building purposes in the region. On the south fork of the American River, Sutter hired another American, James Marshall, to build and operate a sawmill with him.

Photo of Sutter circa 1850

James W. Marshall

Needing workers, Marshall hired former soldiers from the Mormon Battalion who had stayed on in California after the Mexican-American War. Many were in California for religious reasons; they had been part of Brigham Young's trek to the Great Salt Basin in Utah, and they saw the chance to live in California as an opportunity to open more of the west to the Kingdom of Zion.

Many Mormon soldiers had participated in the opening of the "Mormon Corridor," as southern California was called, and they had prepared to return back to newly-risen Salt Lake City, the capital of the Mormon-controlled State of Deseret. If not for an epistle written especially for the Californian Saints, and the placement and influence of a powerful Mormon in San Francisco, the Mormons never would have been present as laborers at Sutter's sawmill on the American River, the place where surface gold was first discovered.[3]

---

[3] The Discovery of Gold in California (California Geological Survey - Gold Discovery)

Mormon laborers worked on Sutter's mill to increase the flow of water into the waterwheel. The digging of dirt, blasting of boulders, and moving of granite made the river's fork deeper and wider. The work also upset the composition of the earth. What happened next was recorded in two sources, long after the event. The first was written by James Marshall in 1857, as he related what happened on January 24, 1848.[4]

> "I used to go down in the morning to see what had been done by the water through the night; and about half past seven o'clock on or about the 19th of January—I am not quite certain of a day, but it was between the 18th and 20th of that month—1848, I went down as usual . . . [near] the lower end [of the mill race], . . . upon the rock, about six inches beneath the surface of the water, I DIS-COVERED THE GOLD. I was entirely alone at the time, I picked up one or two pieces and examined them attentively."[5]

[4] The Discovery of Gold in California (California Geological Survey - Gold Discovery)
[5] M. Guy Bishop, "A Place in History: The Impact of Sutter's Mill Gold Discovery on Henry Bigler," *Nauvoo Journal*, 103-104, James W. Marshall, as quoted in Hutchings California Magazine (Sacramento, [5]California) 2 [November 1857]: 201,
[5]http://mormonhistoricsites.org/wp-content/uploads/2013/05/NJ11.1_Bishop.pdf

But the only way the date had been fully established is through the study of the journal of Henry Bigler, one of the Mormon workmen. Bigler had written, "On January 24th while looking at the race, through which a little water was running, [Marshall] saw something yellow on the bedrock. . . . Just before we quit work for the day Marshall came up and told us he believed he had found a gold mine."[6]

Of course, farmers and carpenters were not authorities on the topic of precious metals, so Sutter and Marshall literally did not yet know what they had on their hands. Marshall explained the initial discovery, which came about as he was investigating the channel of the stream nearby:

> "I picked up one or two pieces and examined them attentively; and having some general knowledge of minerals, I could not call to mind more than two which in any way resembled this, sulphuret of iron, very bright and brittle; and gold, bright, yet malleable. I then tried it between two rocks, and found that it could be beaten into a different shape, but not broken. I then collected four or five pieces and went up to Mr. Scott (who was working at the carpenters bench making the mill wheel) with the pieces in my hand and said, 'I have found it.'
>
> 'What is it?' inquired Scott.
>
> 'Gold,' I answered.
>
> 'Oh! no,' replied Scott, 'That can't be.'
>
> I said,--'I know it to be nothing else.'

---

[6] M. Guy Bishop, "A Place in History: The Impact of Sutter's Mill Gold Discovery on Henry Biggler," *Nauvoo Journal*, 105, [Henry W. Bigler] "Diary of H. W. Bigler in 1847 and 1848," John S. Hittell, ed., [6]Overland Monthly 10 (September 1887): 242, http://mormonhistoricsites.org/wp-content/uploads/2013/05/NJ11.1_Bishop.pdf

The location of Marshall's discovery

Sure enough, Marshall had found gold just days before the Mexican-American war was ending. Marshall brought up his discovery with Sutter, and the men operating the sawmill performed tests to ensure it was gold. Ironically, Sutter wanted to keep the discovery quiet because he was concerned that it would disrupt his plan to farm in the region and make it that much harder for him to claim title to the nearby lands that he wanted.

Naturally, keeping this kind of secret among several people proved impossible. Other workers on Sutter's Mill also began to find gold, and as more and more people found gold, they didn't exactly want to keep cutting wood. When employees from the mill began to turn up in San Francisco and buy goods with gold, newspaperman Samuel Brannan took notice. As a member of the Mormon Church, Brannan dreamed of a western kingdom for the Saints, and Brannan had lucked out. He lived in a location on the bay that, while not strong in geography, could boast a collection of entrepreneurial merchants who supported the vision of San Francisco as a key port city to command finance and capital for a powerful California. When Brannan learned of the discovery of gold from fellow Mormons in his employ, the city of San Francisco was but a dream; people still called the location "Yerba Buena." Sandbars surrounded parts of the city, estuaries were long and marshy places that refused to port ocean-going ships, and banks of fog and wind swept over a dry, hilly peninsula covered in places by dunes.

Brannan

Eventually, Brannan headed to the mill as a representative for the Latter Day Saints, ostensibly to collect tithes from Mormon workers. But when Brannan also found gold near Sutter's Mill, he intended to do exactly what one would expect a writer to do: write about it. There was just one problem; many of the paper's employees had already set off in search of gold themselves. As one biography of Brannan put it, "Brannan moved to New Helvetia, where he opened a store at John Sutter's Fort. When gold was discovered, Brannan owned the only store between San Francisco and the gold fields -- a fact he capitalized on by buying up all the picks, shovels and pans he could find, and then running up and down the streets of San Francisco, shouting 'Gold! Gold on the American River!'"

Like many opportunists, Brannan would make his fortune not by mining gold but by selling goods to the miners. Brannan used news of the discovery of gold at Sutter's Mill as a form of advertisement that allowed him to dominate the mercantile potential of a young California and use the location to stage an economic empire. He found Yerba Buena as a town of huts and dunes and left it a city of San Francisco with shops and brick streets. Imperial San Francisco was born, and it, along with its merchants who sold materials to the first miners, would ultimately command the Gold Rush.[7]

The myth of Brannan waving a bottle of gold in the streets of San Francisco is less important than the impulse of business men just like him to make San Francisco the economic capital of California and the most important city on the West Coast. Their mercantile ambitions ensured that a powerful state would rise around San Francisco, and the population would increase, as the point of entry for thousands of miners to travel to the gold fields in the Northern and Southern Mines.[8]

The *Californian* did, in fact, advertise on March 15, 1848 about the discovery of gold at Sutter's Mill, but the notice received little attention until Brannan's association of merchants backed the news and made it important enough for the first Californians -- not only Californios and Native Americans, but Mexican-American War veterans -- to operate on a low-technological level. As the California Geological Survey explains, these early miners were initially stooped over, immersed in the freezing rivers, and working from sunup to sundown:

> "The crude method of pen-knife and butcher-knife mining soon gave way to more adequate methods of placer mining. The batea, or dish shaped Indian basket, the iron gold pan, and the cradle, which were used to expedite the process of separation of gold and sediment, were soon in evidence. The cradle (or rocker as it was often called) proved to be inefficient because of the loss of many of the small particles, and was soon improved. The new development was the long tom, an elongated, non-rocking cradle in which transverse cleats arrested these small gold particles. Soon, however, the long tom was superseded by sluices of various types."[9]

---

[7] "Map of San Francisco Showing Business Section and Waterfront, 1851 - 1852," http://www.ronhenggeler.com/History/yerba_buena/1851map.htm; The Virtual Museum of the City of San Francisco, "From the 1820s to the Gold Rush," http://www.sfmuseum.org/hist1/early.html; "The Renaming of San Francisco," http://www.sfmuseum.net/hist/name.html

[8] Gold Rush (Part Four: The Legacy), "Businesses, Banks Cashed in by 'Mining the Miners,'" http://www.calgoldrush.com/lb_sets/04business.html

[9] The Discovery of Gold in California (California Geological Survey - Gold Discovery)

A man panning for gold

Sluicing to separate the gold from the dirt and water

Announcement of the discovery of gold

Army officer William Tecumseh Sherman, who would later become a legend during the Civil War, was stationed near San Francisco when gold was discovered, and he wrote of the initial discovery in his memoirs:

"I remember one day, in the spring of 1848, that two men, Americans, came into the office and inquired for the Governor. I asked their business, and one answered that they had just come down from Captain Sutter on special business, and they wanted to see Governor Mason in person. I took them in to the colonel, and left them together. After some time the colonel came to his door and called to me. I went in, and my attention was directed to a series of papers unfolded on his table, in which lay about half an ounce of placer-gold. Mason said to me, "What is that?" I touched it and examined one or two of the larger pieces, and asked, "Is it gold?" Mason asked me if I had ever seen native gold. I answered that, in 1844, I was in Upper Georgia, and there saw some native gold, but it was much finer than this, and it was in phials, or in transparent quills; but I said that, if this were gold, it could be easily tested, first, by its malleability, and next by acids. I took a piece in my teeth, and the metallic lustre was perfect. I then called to the clerk, Baden, to bring an axe and hatchet from the backyard. When these were brought I took the largest piece and beat it out flat, and beyond doubt it was metal, and a pure metal. Still, we attached little importance to the fact, for gold was known to exist at San Fernando, at the south, and yet was not considered of much value.

Colonel Mason then handed me a letter from Captain Sutter, addressed to him, stating that he (Sutter) was engaged in erecting a saw-mill at Coloma, about forty miles up the American Fork, above his fort at New Helvetia, for the general benefit of the settlers in that vicinity; that he had incurred considerable expense, and wanted a 'preëmption' to the quarter-section of land on which the mill was located, embracing the tail-race in which this particular gold had been found. Mason instructed me to prepare a letter, in answer, for his signature. I wrote off a letter, reciting that California was yet a Mexican province, simply held by us as a conquest; that no laws of the United States yet applied to it, much less the land laws or preëmption laws, which could only apply after a public survey. Therefore it was impossible for the Governor to promise him (Sutter) a title to the land; yet, as there were no settlements within forty miles, he was not likely to be disturbed by trespassers. Colonel Mason signed the letter, handed it to one of the gentlemen who had brought the sample of gold, and they departed.

That gold was the first discovered in the Sierra Nevada, which soon revolutionized the whole country, and actually moved the whole civilized world."

Sherman himself eventually saw Sutter's Mill and explained how its operations made it suitable for also mining gold: "Labor was very scarce, expensive, and had to be economized. The mill was built over a dry channel of the river which was calculated to be the tail-race. After arranging his head-race, dam and tub-wheel, he let on the water to test the goodness of his machinery. It worked very well until it was found that the tail-race did not carry off the water fast enough, so he put his men to work in a rude way to clear out the tail-race. They scratched a kind of ditch down the middle of the dry channel, throwing the coarser stones to one side; then, letting on the water again, it would run with velocity down the channel, washing away the dirt, thus saving labor. This course of action was repeated several times, acting exactly like the long Tom afterward resorted to by the miners."

Ironically, the people most responsible for discovering gold were also among the hardest hit by the discovery. Sutter couldn't control the employees on his sawmill once rumors of Marshall's discovery made their way around, as Sherman explained, "Marshall returned to the mill, but could not keep out of his wonderful ditch, and by some means the other men employed there learned his secret. They then wanted to gather the gold, and Marshall threatened to shoot them if they attempted it; but these men had sense enough to know that if "placer"-gold existed at Coloma, it would also be found farther down-stream, and they gradually "prospected" until they reached Mormon Island, fifteen miles below, where they discovered one of the richest placers on earth. These men revealed the fact to some other Mormons who were employed by Captain Sutter at a grist-mill he was building still lower down the American Fork, and six miles above his fort. All of them struck for high wages, to which Sutter yielded, until they asked ten dollars a day, which he refused, and the two mills on which he had spent so much money were never built, and fell into decay." In addition to Sutter's Mill never flourishing, Marshall himself would die penniless, not getting in on the gold rush early enough and then losing money when he did enter the business years down the line.

If anything, the ability to mine surface gold -- placer mining -- required a society to be built up from scratch at it most rudimentary level. While 1849 is often remembered as the year of the Gold Rush, the miners that came the year after the discovery greatly relied upon the people who were already there. The local society boosted the opportunity of gold mining from the beginning, and it required people already in the vicinity to create and maintain the first towns in the Sierra Nevada foothills. The '48ers, as history has called them, created the infrastructure that would support the Gold Rush, which would lure about 300,000 miners when it was all said and done. people at-work in the end. Dale Kassler wrote, "The discovery of gold spawned the stunningly swift development of a sophisticated market-driven economy run by bankers, venture capitalists, importers, experts and merchants of all kind, including many who once had tried their hands at mining. It was an economy that made tycoons out of people like Levi Strauss, a dry-goods merchant from Bavaria, and the slick real estate speculators who bought and sold parcels of land in Sacramento on an almost daily basis. There were corporations established to move people and provisions from San Francisco to Sacramento. There were companies that bought gold dust and companies that minted coins and companies that did both."

While the people near San Francisco quickly began rushing toward the area where gold was discovered, it still took a lot of time for news to travel, and the discovery of gold did not truly lead to a "rush" until the announcement from President James Polk near the end of the year. Victory in the Mexican-American War (1846-1848) had given America a "golden California," and by the end of the year, as if guided by divine providence, the state seemed prepared to live up to its promise. Polk announced to Congress that December:

> "It was known that mines of the precious metals existed to a considerable extent in California at the time of its acquisition. Recent discoveries render it probable that these mines are more extensive and valuable than was anticipated. The accounts of the abundance of gold in that territory are of such an extraordinary character as would scarcely command belief were they not corroborated by the authentic reports of officers in the public service who have visited the mineral district and derived the facts which they detail from personal observation. Reluctant to credit the reports in general circulation as to the quantity of gold, the officer commanding our forces in

California visited the mineral district in July last for the purpose of obtaining accurate information on the subject. His report to the War Department of the result of his examination and the facts obtained on the spot is herewith laid before Congress. When he visited the country there were about 4,000 persons engaged in collecting gold. There is every reason to believe that the number of persons so employed has since been augmented. The explorations already made warrant the belief that the supply is very large and that gold is found at various places in an extensive district of country."[10]

Perhaps the delivery of wealth eased Polk's mind about the decision to forcibly annex California, and the manner in which he led the nation into the Mexican-American War as a whole, but the problems of gold almost immediately destabilized the new American territory. Like employees at Sutter's Mill and Brannan's paper, soldiers deserted their posts, while inflation caused financial distress in the region. Worse, Polk knew that nations from around the world, especially the Pacific Rim, would send miners to claim the riches of California. If the U.S. did not mount a concerted effort to secure the surface riches of the land, the promise of California, which had proved contentious and controversial, would be lost. Thus, the Gold Rush was not just the extraction of a resource, but the creation of a society, ruled by American institutions, that could promote and protect the promise of California, a state poised to represent the most extreme version of the American Dream.[11]

The announcement of the discovery of gold in California and the subsequent gold rush had immediate effects on Americans and the country as a whole, as the California Geological Survey noted, "There were other important consequences, if not always fortunate ones, as a result of the gold rush. It opened the era of modern mining; it hastened the colonization of the West and the suppression and partial elimination of the Indian; it accelerated the expansion of the agricultural frontier by the need for a food supply in the gold area; and it expedited the linking of East and West."[12]

---

[10] American Presidency Project, "James K. Polk, Fourth Annual Message (Dec. 5, 1848), http://www.presidency.ucsb.edu/ws/?pid=29489
[11] American Presidency Project, "James K. Polk, Fourth Annual Message (Dec. 5, 1848), http://www.presidency.ucsb.edu/ws/?pid=29489
[12] The Discovery of Gold in California (California Geological Survey - Gold Discovery)

Chapter 3: The Argonauts

The news of California gold changed communities in the east by the very power of information. People who had initially greeted the news lukewarmly had changed their opinions drastically by the end of 1848, and many of them would now have to decide whether to leave their homes in an effort to find gold, knowing that they would be throwing caution to the wind. The very idea of the journey gave many great pause, as they knew what a trip to California would mean. Jobs and homes would not only be given up, but families as well. It was not just a decision that affected the well-to-do with connections but also the young people who had previously considered settling down in their local communities but now saw the chance to finally leave and take advantage of the tantalizing wealth in the land of California that was ostensibly available to anyone who could find gold.

This seemed to make the decision much easier, yet the men and women who left created novel solutions to solve the problem, and formed companies that, at first, were recreations of their communities. As Malcolm Rohrbough explained, "Those who determined to go often did so in a 'company' with their friends and neighbors. The company was, in truth, often a replica of the local community from which they came...The company formed and the officers chosen...Men who had been tied to labor on farms and shops suddenly found themselves officer in companies preparing to depart for California. On ethem gell such solemn duties as victualling, gathering uniforms and arms, and drafting a constitution. The hum and buzz of activity transformed their communities, and they became the envy of all those who had wished to go but decided to remain."[13]

While many left for California for personal gain, others clothed their journey in tones of patriotism and religious duties, thinking they were accomplishing the task for the goal of extending American power, society, and even the English language and the true Christian religion -- Protestantism. The fanfare that saw them off expressed itself in terms of a mighty crusade that would sweep away the former Mexican masters (and the implied laziness these Americans associated with Mexicans), as well as removing the Catholic faith brought to the land by the Spanish. In that respect, gold fever acted as a part of Manifest Destiny, and the wharves that saw the ships off to the West were carrying people who convinced themselves they were not leaving simply for their families and personal gain but for a higher cause. They would venture forth to continue the American Dream; and riches in California would be the engine of that desire.

These sentiments were on display in one of the most famous primary accounts written by a miner, one written by a man with the last name Shufelt. His letters back home have been archived by the Library of Congress, but the results of his venture to California remain unknown, as does his first name. Shufelt wrote home, "I have left those that I love as my own life behind and risked everything and endured many hardships to get here. I want to make enough to live easier and do some good with, before I return."

Though they are known as Forty-Niners today, at first the people who headed for California were known as the Argonauts, a reference to the old Greek myth about Jason and the Argonauts, and the fact that most people sailed to California instead of attempting to go over land. For those who did trek across the continent, their travels not only took them to a land few Americans had ever seen but across lands Americans knew little about, yet had heard of. For the ones who chose to go by ship, either around South America and Cape Horn, their stops took them to the Deep South, and Argonauts also came into contact with the reliquaries of the old Spanish Empire, Cuba, Argentina, Colombia, and Peru. They saw the gothic cathedrals and marveled at the near-antiquity of the "other" Americas.

Those who didn't want to sail further south to the tip of South America could choose to cross the Panamanian isthmus in the "Nueva Granada," later to be called Colombia. However, many who attempted that had their trip shortened when they came into contact with swamps full of

---

[13] Rohrbough, "'No Boys Play:' Migration and Settlement in Early Gold Rush California," *Rooted in Barbarous Soil: People, Culture, and Community in Gold Rush California*, 29.

malaria and a population that recoiled at the cultural insensitivity of the "raza yanqui." At the same time, the contact of Argonauts with Latin America would be important for later events in the coming decades.

Shufelt was one of the ones who sailed around South America, and he wrote home:

"(We) proceeded up the river in canoes rowed by the natives, and enjoyed the scenery & howling of the monkeys & chattering of Parrots very much. We pitched our tents at Gorgona & most of our party stayed there several weeks. S. Miller & myself went on to Panama to look out for a chance to get up to San Francisco. Of our ill success you have probably been informed & consequently of our long stay there, & of the deaths in our party. Yes, here Mr. Crooker, J. Miller & L. Alden yielded up their breath to God who gave it.

After many delays & vexations, we at length took passage on a German ship & set sail again on our journey to the Eldorado of the west. We went south nearly to the Equator, then turned west, the weather was warm, the winds light & contrary for our course. Our ship was a slow sailer & consequently our passage was long & tedious. One of the sailors fell from the rigging into the water & it was known that he could not swim, so the excitement was great. Ropes, planks and every thing that could be got hold of was thrown to him. He caught a plank & got on it, a boat was lowered & soon they had him on board again. He was much frightened, but not much hurt. We had one heavy squall of wind & rain, that tore the sails & broke some of the yards in pieces, & gave us a quick step motion to keep upon our feet, but soon all was right again & we were ploughing through the gentle Pacific at the rate of ten knots per hour.

On the 85th day out we hove in sight of an object that greatly attracted our attention & ere long the green hills of San Francisco bay began to show their highest points, & soon we were gliding smoothly along between them, down the bay, & when the order came to let go anchor, we brought up directly in front of the City amidst a fleet of vessels, of all kinds & sizes."

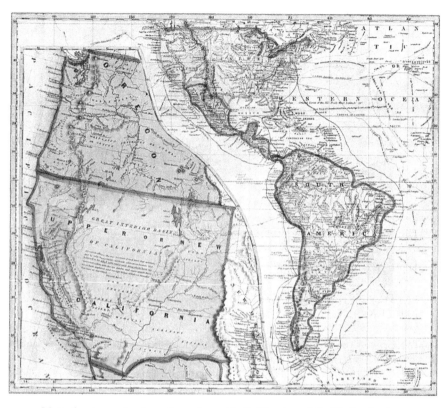

Map of water routes from the east coast to California and the Mother Lode

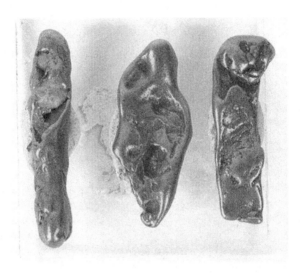

Gold nuggets found in the Mother Lode, Tuolumne County

Overland travelers faced a more dramatic journey, as the trip across the continent required a departure date in mid-May to reach the foothills of the Sierra Nevada mountains by the beginning of October, which was necessary to beat the first winter snows. This would be the first time large groups of Americans saw "the fabled symbols of the American West: the huge herds of buffalo, the dangerous Plains Indians tribes (feared but rarely seen), the towering peaks of the Rockies and the Sierra Nevada, the national monuments of Chimney Rock, Fort Laramie, and the Mormon enclave around the Great Salt Lake."[14]

All travelers, whether they arrived by sea or land, disembarked at three urban centers: San Francisco, Stockton, and Sacramento. Most miners decided to stick together, typically in groups of seven to eight people, and this personal arrangement would be all most miners ever knew. They bought their equipment together, they lived together, and they took care of each other in the camps and in the field. As Rohrbough wrote, their existence was one of intense hardship and intimacy.

> "The basic unit of work in the California Gold Rush -- at least for the first half-dozen years -- was the human body. The hard, repetitive labor of digging, carrying, and washing was often done in swift, ice-cold, moving water...Contrasting with the icy water of the snowmelt of the watercourses was the heat of the California summer, beating down on the bars and into the still

[14] Rohrbough, "'No Boys Play:' Migration and Settlement in Early Gold Rush California," *Rooted in Barbarous Soil: People, Culture, and Community in Gold Rush California*, 36.

canyons. The work was exhausting...So during the long work days that stretched into a long mining season, gold seekers drove themselves forward on a daily basis through a combination of restless energy, hope, self-interest, group loyalty, and sometimes desperation."[15]

Shufelt described his initial attempts to find gold:

"We hired an ox team to carry our baggage & started for this place then called Hangtown, from the fact that three persons had been hung here for stealing & attempting to murder. Ten miles from the river we passed Sutters fort, an old looking heap of buildings surrounded by an high wall of unburnt brick, & situated in the midst of a pleasant fertile plain, covered with grass and a few scattering oaks, with numerous tame cattle & mules. We walked by the wagon & at night cooked our suppers, rolled our blankets around us & lay down to rest on the ground, with nothing but the broad canopy of the heavens over us & slept soundly without fear or molestation. After leaving the plains we passed over some hills that looked dry & barren being burnt up by the sun & the long droughts that we have here. We reached this place at night on the fourth day, & in the morning found ourselves in the midst of the diggings, being surrounded by holes dug.

We pitched our tents, shouldered our picks & shovels & with pan in hand sallied forth to try our fortunes at gold digging. We did not have very good success being green at mining, but by practice & observation we soon improved some, & found a little of the shining metal. "

It is found along the banks of the streams & in the beds of the same, & in almost every little ravine putting into the streams. And often from 10 to 50 ft. from the beds up the bank. We sometimes have to dig several feet deep before we find any, in other places all the dirt & clay will pay to wash, but generally the clay pays best. If there is no clay, then it is found down on the rock. All the lumps are found on the rock--& most of the fine gold. We tell when it will pay by trying the dirt with a pan. This is called prospecting here. If it will pay from six to 12 1/2 pr pan full, then we go to work. Some wash with cradles some with what is called a tom & various other fixings. But I like the tom best of any thing that I have seen.

It is a box or trough about 8 or 9 feet long, some 18 in. wide & from 5 to 6 in. high, with an iron sieve in one end punched with 1/2 in. holes. Underneath this is placed a ripple or box with two ripples across it. The tom is then placed in an oblique position, the water is brought on by means of a hose. The dirt, stone, clay & all is then thrown in & stirred with a shovel until the water runs clear, the gold &

---

[15] Rohrbough, "'No Boys Play:' Migration and Settlement in Early Gold Rush California," *Rooted in Barbarous Soil: People, Culture, and Community in Gold Rush California*, 40-41.

finer gravel goes through the sieve & falls in the under box & lodges above the ripples. Three men can wash all day without taking this out as the water washes the loose gravel over and all the gold settles to the bottom. One man will wash as fast as two can pick & shovel it in, or as fast as three rockers or cradles."

Just as important were the living situations many found themselves in. The groups of miners shared every household task and had to cover the previously unknown sphere of domesticity that had usually been reserved to women back home. As a result miners who prided themselves on their masculine imperviousness to physical pain also had to double as cooks, seamstresses, and nurses for each other. Far from entering a recognizable world, they entered one defined by new methods of living and brand new cultures as well. Whites were hardly the only ones participating in the rush.

Shufelt, who lived in a small cabin with half a dozen other miners, explained the living conditions in a letter:

"Many, very many, that come here meet with bad success & thousands will leave their bones here. Others will lose their health, contract diseases that they will carry to their graves with them. Some will have to beg their way home, & probably one half that come here will never make enough to carry them back. But this does not alter the fact about the gold being plenty here, but shows what a poor frail being man is, how liable to disappointments, disease & death.

There is a good deal of sin & wickedness going on here, Stealing, lying, Swearing, Drinking, Gambling & murdering. There is a great deal of gambling carried on here. Almost every public House is a place for Gambling, & this appears to be the greatest evil that prevails here. Men make & lose thousands in a night, & frequently small boys will go up & bet $5 or 10 (Equivalent to $115-$225 today) -- & if they lose all, go the next day & dig more. We are trying to get laws here to regulate things but it will be very difficult to get them executed."

Chapter 4: Las Californias

Though it's often forgotten now, at the time gold was discovered in California, whites were a minority in the extreme, outnumbered by Native Americans at a rate of about 35:1 alone. That didn't even account for the Mexicans in the area. As a result, white miners came to a California formed by regions closest to it, and in no way resembling the American culture found further east on the same continent.

California did not belong to the Atlantic world that most miners had come from; the Pacific Ocean provided different flavors from Asia, Australia, the Pacific Northwest, and South America, and the camps the miners created only added to the present mix. This soon became apparent in the choice of foods they ate, from Mexican to Chilean to Chinese. Their choice of pleasurable tastes also involved the diverse selection of people from different cultures, as miners grew enamored of the different women and men in the camps, expressing desires to have sexual relations with Chileans, Mexicans, Native Americans, and with the other men too. In addition to a general lack of women in the area, many of the miners were willing to stretch gender roles and activities by engaging in relationships that subverted the usual divisions between relationships defined by male/female and man/woman. Simply put, more men than women occupied the camps, and the geographic patterns of settlement based on migration trails also made white men a minority, at least initially. As Susan Lee Johnson wrote, "This was especially true of men who lived and worked in the Southern Mines, that region in the Sierra Nevada foothills tributary to the San Joaquin River...the Southern Mines, by far the most demographically diverse of California's mining areas. At the end of the 1850s, for example, immigrants from outside the United State -- along with some African Americans and non-California Indians, such as Cherokee -- outnumbered Anglo Americans there."[16]

Geography explained the first wave of miners to immigrate to California. It was not the east coast and its Americans who came first but people from Peru, Chile, and Mexicans who arrived by ship and land. Settlers from Oregon and British Columbia -- Oregon Country -- and further abroad from Australia and New Zealand soon arrived as well. Furthermore, Hawaiians from the islands entered the minefields too. Yet even these groups were preceded by the Native Californians and the "Californio" Mexican colonists. Far from finding a place unformed, Americans merely added to the culture of the place; and the camps and their locations in California explained the differences of the world of early California. Sucheng Chan noted:

> "A significant number of British Columbians, many of whom were British-born, and Oregonians dug for the precious metal in the Trinity-Klamath-Shasta Region, which they had traversed as they journeyed southward. American Forty-Niners who had cross the Great Plains and the Rocky Mountains dominate the Northern Mines in Plumas, Butte, Sierra, Yuba, Nevada, Placer, El Dorado, and Amador counties because southern branch of the California Trail cut through the Sierra Nevada at the Carson Pass and Donner Pass, which led to the Northern Mines. The largest contingent of Latin Americans prospected in the Southern Mines -- in Calaveras, Tuolumne, and Mariposa counties -- because as they trekked northward they reached that area first."[17]

---

[16] Johnson, *Rooted in Barbarous Soil: People, Culture, and Community in Gold Rush California*, "'My Own Private Life': Toward a History of Desire in Gold Rush California," 316.

[17] Chan, *Rooted in Barbarous Soil: People, Culture, and Community in Gold Rush California*," A People of Exceptional Character": Ethnic Diversity, Nativism, and Racism in the California Gold Rush," 54-55.

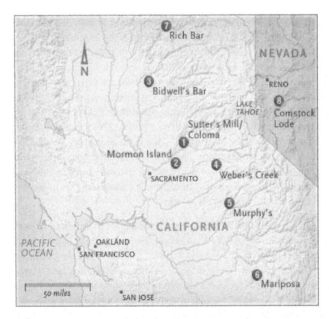

Early miner camps

The Californios belonged to the first generation of Mexican colonists to be born in *Las Californias*, with dreams of a more democratic state and a stronger, less-mercantalist economy. The coming of the Americans and the Gold Rush were initially things that the Mexican colonists wanted to turn to their advantage. They had learned to recognize the U.S.'s previous rehearsals for invasion, but the feeling grew among the Mexican elites on the Californian frontier that the future prosperity of Alta California lay with negotiated relationships with the American settlers. Such a plan would remove the biggest threats to Californio aspirations: the Church and the military. The Franciscans had successfully laid claim to Alta California following the Sacred Expedition of 1769-1770, but the establishment of the religious order's 21 missions and the presidio-based colonial military proved a challenge until the liberal reforms of the Mexican nation following the collapse of Emperor Agustin Iturbide "empire" in 1830s Mexico. With that, the Californios finally broke the power of the Franciscan order and took advantage of the secularization program that targeted the missions of Alta California.

The Californios longed for a Mexico that granted them entrepreneurial freedom, which had languished during Spain's calculated isolation of the Californias, treating the territory as a mere frontier buffer zone against Native American and American invasions. But after the removal of the Franciscan power in the missions, the Californios not only expanded their already-large estates but were able to intercede in the lives of Natives who the mission priests had claimed dominion over. Though the Californios professed a liberal treatment of the natives, the intimate relationship they fostered with the natives turned oppressive in its paternalism. The Native Americans provided a function to the ranching economy of the Californio baronial estates, working in most cases for the bare pay of subsistence, while their overlords looked lazily after their education and forced them to adopt Christianity and a European lifestyle. The Californio lords would take advantage of this labor arrangement during the initial stage of the Gold Rush, when the ranch owners traded the natives food for their labor in the gold fields.[18]

The Californios stood to gain the most from the Gold Rush because of their long-standing attempts to remain autonomous from the central government of Mexico. They not only battled with government officers; families in the northern and southern Alta California battled one another for control of the provincial government. In 1844, two years before the Mexican-American War, the two sections of the state united against the Mexican governor, Michetorena, and two years later at the Battle of La Providencia, defeated the governor, who then left Alta California. Mexico no longer controlled Alta California, which would operate like an independent nation until the end of the American-led Bear Flag Rebellion, when the U.S. Army finally seized control of the state. By 1848, Alta California's enjoyed a state of de facto independence, though the region lay divided by rival regimes in the north and south.[19]

The Californios in the south ultimately ended up doing better than their northern compatriots due to the impact of the Gold Rush on the San Francisco Bay Area. For a period of time, the cattle of the southern ranches became sought after, in order to feed the miners. The Californios successfully led cattle drives up the coast and San Joaquin Valley to the buyer's market of their beef. For a period of years in the early Gold Rush, the Californios near the Mission of San Diego enjoyed the greatest financial success. However, the exchange rate of gold and spending habits drastically reordered their world and caused an eventual decline. For one, the greater deal has been placed on the sudden wealth the Californios had because of the Gold Rush. They spent exorbitantly, as some historians claim; and this might be true, but the arrival of thousands of new Californians made products scarce, driving up costs for goods that everyone struggled to pay, Californios included.[20]

In retrospect, the most significant development that changed the financial fortunes of the Californios involved the re-alignment of the commercial center of California from the south to the north in San Francisco. Suddenly marginalized, and bested by later competitors, the Californios of the south could not engage in any profitable trade due to high freight costs. This ultimately impoverished them and left them financially vulnerable to the long period of litigation

---

[18] Rose Marie Beebe and Robert M. Senkewicz, *Chonicles of Early California, 1535-1846: Lands of Promise and Despair*, 341, 345, 375, 390; Californios, "Californios, A People and a Culture," http://www.californios.us/ca/

[19] The California State Military Museum, "Spanish and Mexican California: Battle of La Providencia (Second Battle of Cahuenga Pass), http://www.militarymuseum.org/LaProvidencia.html

[20] The Journal of San Diego History, "The Decline of the Californios: The Case of San Diego (1846-1856)," http://www.sandiegohistory.org/journal/75summer/decline.htm

that followed American conquest. The loss of land from the Board of Land Commissioners made it nearly impossible for them to turn their full attention to the opportunities of the Gold Rush. Years spent in court defending their land claims finally bankrupted most of the ranchers, who were forced to sell their property to pay legal costs.[21]

The large number of merchant vessels in San Francisco's harbor is quickly apparent in this picture, taken circa 1850-1851

---

[21] The Journal of San Diego History, "The Decline of the Californios: The Case of San Diego (1846-1856)," http://www.sandiegohistory.org/journal/75summer/decline.htm

Chapter 5: Dealing with Demographics

Roy D. Graves' illustration of Chinese miners

The flow of Chinese immigrants increased dramatically in 1852, sparked in large part by a crop failure in southern China that caused the custom houses in San Francisco to swell with 20,026 Chinese arrivals. Even more Chinese came as news reached China about the apparent ease of mining in California. By the end of the decade, ⅕ of the population of the Southern Mines consisted of Chinese miners. Chinese miners would become known as the most industrious and tireless of the miners, finding gold in claims that previous owners had thought depleted and persisting in mining an area far longer than others who eventually left the fields altogether.

However, other miners reacted to their presence negatively, and in some cases Chinese miners had their camps violently attacked. The state government attempted to rectify the problem through the creation of a second Miner's Tax, but unfortunately this only seemed to accelerate other miners' attacks on Chinese camps. Reports in the same year indicated that an epidemic of robberies hit the immigrant miners from China, close to 200 alone, along with a series of murders.

All of this can partly explain why the Chinese decided to diversify and choose occupations that did not put them into open competition with white American miners. Another reason, and one closer to the financial windfalls that occurred during the Gold Rush, is explained by the chance for profit in the mercantile and service industries. The Chinese moved into the laundry business, other domestic services, and later railroad building, all of which necessarily thrived as the population in the region boomed. Taking some of these businesses was also acts of gender subversion, at least by the standards of European Americans -- men just did not undertake careers usually thought of as domestic chores. For the Chinese, necessity and less aversion to these jobs brought profits, but these jobs also created more feelings of alienation between the Argonauts and the foreign-born miners.[22]

The Chinese could never overcome the legal obstacles towards true success and acceptance in Californian society during the Gold Rush, and the discriminatory procedures that prevented Chinese immigrants from full protection under the law would have had little power if not for the state apparatus that legitimized and enforced racism, namely the California Supreme Court.[23] As one historian explained, "In the case *People v. Hall*, the California Supreme Court reversed the conviction of George Hall and two other white men who had murdered a Chinese man. Hall and his companions had been convicted based on testimony of some Chinese witnesses. In its reversal the court extended the California law that African Americans and Native Americans could not testify in court to include the Chinese. The reversal made it impossible to prosecute violence against Chinese immigrants."[24]

Demographically, the numbers of blacks and Chinese also contributed to the diversity of the gold fields and the culture of the earliest days of California, which became a state in 1850. Black people had come from Latin America, but the largest number of them had come from the U.S., and 5,000 African-Americans lived in California by 1852. The largest numbers came as slaves of Southern masters who intended to personally use them in the gold fields or rent them out as laborers for other men, but some free blacks were drawn by the allure of gold themselves.

The presence of African-Americans also had a major influence on what kind of society California would be. The presence of blacks lay at the heart of the constitutional convention of the state of California, because slavery was a highly contentious issue at the time. With so much new territory to carve into states, the balance of Congressional power became a hot topic for the nation, and it had been since the people of Missouri sought to be admitted to the Union in 1819 with slavery being legal in the new state. While Congress was dealing with that, Alabama was admitted in December 1819, creating an equal number of free states and slave states. Thus, allowing Missouri to enter the Union as a slave state would disrupt the balance.

---

[22] The Gold Rush, "People and Events: Chinese Immigrants and the Gold Rush,"
http://www.pbs.org/wgbh/amex/goldrush/peopleevents/p_chinese.html
[23] The Gold Rush, "People and Events: Chinese Immigrants and the Gold Rush,"
http://www.pbs.org/wgbh/amex/goldrush/peopleevents/p_chinese.html
[24] Chinese Immigrants and the Gold Rush

Congress ultimately got around this issue by establishing what became known as the Missouri Compromise. Legislation was passed that admitted Maine as a free state, thus balancing the number once Missouri joined as a slave state. Moreover, slavery would be excluded from the Missouri Territory north of the parallel 36°30' north, which was the southern border of Missouri itself. As a slave state, Missouri would obviously serve as the lone exception to that line.

The Missouri Compromise of 1820 staved off the crisis for the time being, but by setting a line that excluded slave states above the parallel, it would also become incredibly contentious. After the Mexican-American War ended in 1848, the sectional crisis was brewing like never before, with California and the newly-acquired Mexican territory now ready to be organized into states. The country was once again left trying to figure out how to do it without offsetting the slave-free state balance. With the new territory acquired in the Mexican-American War, pro and anti-slavery groups were at an impasse. The Whig Party supported the Wilmot Proviso, which would have banned slavery in all territory acquired from Mexico, but the slave states would have none of it. Even after Texas was annexed as a slave state, the enormous new territory would doubtless contain many other new states, and the North hoped to limit slavery as much as possible in the new territories.

Delegates to the California conventions expressed concerns about the presence of slaves in the language of other anti-slavery people, who saw the institution as a threat to free labor and the power of large businesses. But at the same time, there were so many advocates for slavery in the convention, mostly from southern California, that at one point there was a serious conversation about splitting up California into two states, one free and one slave. That said, the real weight of the conversation, which explained the crisis at the convention, revolved around whether or not any blacks should be allowed to enter the state at all.

California effectively created exceptions to the legal system in order to control the numbers of blacks and Chinese. While the state did not bar African-Americans from entering, it did prevent them from taking legal action to protect themselves from discrimination. Blacks mined, but they could never really live the lives they wanted to in a "free California." Discrimination was much more severe against the Chinese, as the Miners Tax meant their profits as laborers were severely curtailed. As for the matter of allowing the Chinese to enter the state, exclusion would come much later during the final stages of the Gold Rush, when, once again, class issues and ideas about the corruption of big business would come into play. Nevertheless, Chinese did face "commutative tolls" for entering the state. For the Chinese and African Americans, social stratification hardened, and race truly determined how certain groups labored, where they lived, and what rights they had in the courts. Chan explains:

> "This process of stratification had begun during the Spanish and Mexican periods, but it accelerate with the Gold Rush. The creation of such a hierarchy involved five sub-processes vis-a-vis peoples of color: the *exploitation* of their labor, the *denial* of their civil rights, the *aversion* of social contracts with them,

the *deprivation* of their chances for upward mobility, and the insistence on *deference* in the behavior toward the European American majority. The rapid emergence of such an unequal society -- one that goes against the professed American creed -- is one of the darker legacies of the Gold Rush."[25]

Of course, there was also the matter of Native Americans, of which there were upwards of about 150,000 in California. The Native Americans of California faced intense hatred from the Forty-Niners, initially due to their labor relationship with the Californio barons. Some of the first white Americans to mine gold came from Oregon Country; and as they moved south into the Klamath Mountains of Northern California, they encountered the first Californio ranches, where landowners used natives as laborers for the mining of gold. The sight of Indian workers, working mostly for subsistence and not pay, enraged the Oregonians because the institution of work the Californios used had the appearance of slavery.

The removal of Native Americans from California was harshest in the north; over the course of about 12 years, the population went from 150,000 Native Americans in 1848 to 35,000 in 1860. This coincided with the destruction of the economic power of the Californios, who relied upon the native workforce to mine gold, as well as the new tactic of the federal government to relocate natives to reservations. At first, the state passed laws that allowed miners to conscript natives as indentured servants. Then the young government encouraged private militias and individual citizens to play a role in the removal of Native Americans in California.

The removal of Native Americans had several benefits for the Forty-Niners. It opened up more mining areas to them and removed a lot of competition. Not surprisingly, the same policy of removal happened near the Southern Mines in central and southern California, as white settlers wanted the 7.5 percent of California's land area that treaties had set aside for Native Americans. Squatters also moved onto reservation lands in the hopes of securing parcels that gave them access to the foothills of the Sierras, where the mining took place. Except for the surrender of Modoc resisters, who moved onto reservations after defeat at the hands of the U.S. Army, the Native Americans were forcibly removed until most tribes existed as only a few bands.

Perhaps not surprisingly, the groups that prospered in the initial stage of the Gold Rush were the ones that were geographically closer than any group, mainly Mexicans from the state of Sonora, the Californios from Alta California, and the Mormon pioneers from "Deseret" (later to be known as the territory of Utah). These groups stood in the best position to prosper from the mining of gold. Their experience with the terrain and the type of mining put them in the best position, but they also proved invaluable to the other miners for the level of expertise and techniques they would bring to the mining of gold in California. The Sonorans' style of mining was not the method most people associate with the Gold Rush, placer (surface) mining in rivers

[25] Chan, *Rooted in Barbarous Soil: People, Culture, and Community in Gold Rush California*," A People of Exceptional Character": Ethnic Diversity, Nativism, and Racism in the California Gold Rush," 79.

using pans. Instead, the Sonorans used "dry mining." The California Geological Survey explains, "As a method of mining it was simple, crude and inefficient, but it had the advantage of being inexpensive. After the pay dirt was dug, it was sun dried on a large canvas and then pulverized into dust. The next operation was to throw the dirt by the panful into the air in order to allow the wind to blow away the lighter elements and to let the gold dust fall back into the pan. Thus the old agricultural procedure of winnowing was the first method used extensively in California mining; for not only was it used in the Los Angeles area, but also it was introduced by many of these same Sonorans into the mines of the Sierra Nevada after 1848."[26]

The creation of the state of California during the Gold Rush meant the young state was forced to contend with the Californios, who owned a lot of land but engaged in a form of economy that left them nearly destitute in a region that now swelled with the wealth of the riches dug out of the earth. The Gold Rush gave the ranch barons in the south a significant boost, but they eventually became impoverished, and most lost their lands as the economy transformed into one where whites became increasingly involved in the mercantile business. As men like Samuel Brannan determined, commerce was the real "gold" to be found in California during the Gold Rush.[27]

---

[26] The Discovery of Gold in California (California Geological Survey - Gold Discovery)

[27] Sandos, "'Because he is a liar and a thief': Conquering the Residents of 'Old' California, 1850-1880," *Rooted in Barbarous Soil: People, Culture and Community in Gold Rush California.*

Illustration depicting whites, Native Americans, and blacks mining gold together

If harmony existed in the California gold fields of 1848, the arrival of the Forty-Niners, the first large wave of Argonauts, changed all that. They noticed the supremacy of knowledge by the Spanish-speaking miners, especially the successful techniques of the Mexicans from the state of Sonora, who had mined in Mexico and in southern California and could extract large quantities of gold in low-running streams or dry hillsides. American arrivals framed their outrage with these miners in terms of class antagonism, for many believed that the Spanish Californios were elites who benefitted from the labor of natives or the Sonorans, who they described as peasants working on the behest of Mexican mine owners back in Mexico. To American Argonauts, many of whom belonged to the Democratic Party, this appeared to violate egalitarian principles that they intended to bring to California. These social goals were expressed by attempts at creating rules for mining that practiced American social mores and ethics based on free enterprise and democracy. Chan explained how a system of land claims was quickly set up, "Each individual could hold only one claim, except for the person who made the find, who was entitled to two claim. The claim had to be officially recorded an elected recorder. To hold a claim, a miner had to work it a specified number of days per specified time period. Thus, miner enjoyed only usufructuary rights over their claim, with disputes settled at miners' meeting or the recorder of alcalde [mayor]."[28]

Ultimately, the strongest current of hatred involved feelings of racism cloaked in U.S. nationalism. The Forty-Niners felt that since the U.S. had conquered the territory from Mexico, citizens of the nation that controlled California owned full rights to the land, not immigrants from other nations. On top of that, many of the miners had been supporters of the Mexican-American War or even veterans of the fighting, which made them feel even more entitled to California and its gold. There's also no doubt many saw the presence of Catholic, Spanish-speaking, brown skinned people as anathema to the creation of a free, democratic, and industrious California.

The Forty-Niners responded with violence, and then laws, to try to keep foreign miners out of the gold fields. It was not uncommon for white miners to attack non-whites, especially when the 1850 Foreign Miners' Tax gave them the impression that more acts of violence were permitted by law. Eventually, the pressures of Argonauts appeared to pay off, as more Latino miners were expelled from the southern mines, and an exodus resulted later on. However, this attempt proved partially short-lived, as merchants from the region began to lose money without the presence of miners and their gold.

This led to a repeal of the tax, but that did not bring an end to the discrimination. Race played an even larger role in the attempts by Forty-Niners to expel Chinese immigrants and African-Americans from the fields. This was largely because the nature of mining had changed from surface mining to more capital-intensive systems of extracting the gold, such as river, deep shaft or quartz, and hydraulic mining; and cheap labor was needed by the mining corporations.

The use of taxes and violence was facilitated by the fact that California was so far away from the rest of the nation, because establishing a society based on the search and extraction of mineral wealth in a wilderness area created profound problems for San Francisco and California that had far-reaching social consequences. The founders of the city and state were, in every sense of the word, on a quest for riches, and they wanted to promote and sustain this enterprise by a careful mix of regulation and laissez faire. In addition to racial tensions, there was also a tension between government and businesses that invested in the development of the state.

In this kind of environment, San Francisco and the gold fields naturally became a place fraught with cultural diversity and a propensity for violence and lawlessness. The wildness of California does not suggest that the new society did not possess cultural expressions of civil life, as San Francisco did serve as cultural hub of transmission of different clubs, cooperatives, and associations for the promotion of civic life, such as the arts and education, and San Francisco had municipal organizations that would, at least in theory, improve society. However, San Francisco,

---

[28] Chan, *Rooted in Barbarous Soil: People, Culture, and Community in Gold Rush California*," A People of Exceptional Character": Ethnic Diversity, Nativism, and Racism in the California Gold Rush," 59.
28

as an urban center, demonstrated the types of extremes that one would expect of a society based off the dream of instant financial dreams. For the majority that suffered a bust instead of a boom, the failures and disappointments resulted in political upheaval, economic uncertainty, and cycles of violence.[29]

By any measure, these were the conditions of vigilantism in a state with a full constitution that possessed the institutions of a republic but denied civil rights to Californios, Native Americans, Latinos, Hawaiians, and Asians. In a climate where civil rights were easily sidestepped, the rise of violence became its own form of civil development, because the violence was not always random and irrational. There would prove to be a great deal of organization and thought behind the use of force to make sure everyone obeyed the legal rights set forth by the state's constitution.[30]

In his seminal study of American westward expansion and the process of state-making, the notion of the frontier, as explained by Frederick Jackson Turner in 1890, was one of American self-rule and enterprise. This helps explains how California was afflicted in its efforts to self-organize during the Gold Rush, as pointed out by Mary Floyd Williams:

> "It was the multiplicity of revolutionary associations, and the ease with which they might run into the form taken by the Vigilance Committees of the far West, that led even so ardent a follower of revolutionary principles as Patrick Henry to declare in 1786 regarding the defenseless condition of the western frontier, "that protection which is the best and general object of social compact is withdrawn, and the people, thus consigned to destruction, will naturally form associations, disgraceful as they are destructive of government."[31]

While the "Wild West" has long been romanticized, a more accurate portrayal of the American frontier is one about the way men and women joined extralegal organizations to support and enforce the law in the federal territories and new states. In many cases, citizens defined themselves as "regulators," considering themselves a contingency in the event that the legal systems in a state suffered from corruption. Naturally, these extralegal organizations weren't afraid to use violence, justifying their actions by claiming the lack of authorities in the area left it up to them. Put simply, the regulators were vigilantes.[32]

In the case of San Francisco and California during the Gold Rush, instances of political corruption did give rise to vigilantism, but the presence of so-called "law and order" groups, ironically, provoked an extralegal response from San Francisco's business leaders, who feared

---

[29] Ohlone College, "Gold Rush and California Statehood,"
http://www.ohlone.edu/instr/english/elc/engl163/goldrush.html
[30] Gold Fever, "Law, Order, and Justice for Some," http://museumca.org/goldrush/fever16.html;
[31] Mary Floyd Williams, *History of the San Francisco Committee of the Vigilance of 1851*, 13-14, quoted from Turner, F.J, "Western State-Making," *American Historical Review*, 1 (1895-1896), 265-266.
[32] Mary Floyd Williams, *History of the San Francisco Committee of the Vigilance of 1851*

that vigilante groups threatened the democratic and economic health of the state. Violence took the form of racist attacks on foreigners and non-whites who worked in the gold fields, and in these cases, "law and order" groups were seen as wanton, uncontrollable groups by the elites, despite the claim by Forty-Niners that immigrant miners did not obey the laws that governed gold mining claims. Whether or not this was true, the perception of vigilantism's threat to democracy could not be ignored. When gangs of unemployed miners attacked non-white miners, business leaders realized it threatened the civic order that businessmen needed to thrive. Order had to inhabit a region that produced favorable outcomes for the creation and sustainability of wealth.[33]

The Vigilance Committees of 1851 and 1856 should not viewed as the actions of men on the margins of society, but as the organization of men from the business community of San Francisco who had little faith in the men who occupied political office in the city. They had even less faith in the "law and order" forces that regulated the mining camps in the countryside.[34] The Vigilance Committee announced:

> "WHEREAS it has become apparent to the citizens of San Francisco, that there is no security for life and property, either under the regulations of society as it at present exists, or under the law as now administered; *Therefore* the citizens, whose names are hereunto attached, do unit themselves into an association for the maintenance of the peace and good order of society, and the preservation of the lives and property of the citizens of San Francisco, and do bind ourselves, each unto the other, to do and perform every lawful act for the maintenance of law and order, and to sustain the laws when faithfully and properly administered; but we are determined that no thief, burglar, incendiary or assassin, shall escape punishment, either by the quibbles of the law, the insecurity of prisons, the carelessness or corruption of the police, or a laxity of those who pretend to administer justice."[35]

---

[33] *The Examiner*, "San Francisco Law and Order Forces Defeated," http://www.examiner.com/article/san-francisco-law-and-order-forces-defeated; "Vigilante Justice in the Gold Mines," http://www.examiner.com/article/vigilante-justice-the-mines; History Engine, "Crime and Instant Justice in Gold Rush California," http://historyengine.richmond.edu/episodes/view/5127; Calisphere, 1848-1856: Gold Rush Era, "Murder and Mayhem," http://www.calisphere.universityofcalifornia.edu/themed_collections/subtopic1a.html; SF Genealogy: San Francisco History, "The Annals of San Francisco (Part three: The Hounds), http://www.sfgenealogy.com/sf/history/hbann3-1.htm

[34] Maritime Heritage Project, "The Vigilance Committee," http://www.maritimeheritage.org/vips/vigilance.html

[35] Maritime Heritage Project, "The Vigilance Committee," http://www.maritimeheritage.org/vips/vigilance.html

Of these men, Samuel Brannan served as the most important member, and founder, of the first committee. Brannan employed citizens as private "safety committees" to round up the criminal element in San Francisco and its environs, negate the deleterious effects of politicians they deemed ineffective against corruption, and judge and execute all peoples guilty of acts that threatened the civil health of the municipality and the state. Brannan, along with his business associates, presided, either directly or indirectly, over the arrest, tribunals, and corporal punishment of residents of California. This not only took the form of public trials and executions but even the creation of private armies -- sharpshooter brigades -- who engaged in paramilitary operations against vigilante forces inside and outside the city. Gangs of criminals, like the "Sydney Ducks" and bands of anti-foreigner nativists, the Hounds, were destroyed or exiled from the city. Later, safety committees raided illegal gambling and opium dens in San Francisco to police the moral behavior of a city that had grown more worldly and uncontrollable than the city boosters were comfortable with.[36]

Despite the efforts of vigilance committees, vigilantism was part and parcel of an unregulated society born out of an impulse to get rich quick. After all, mining laws actually encouraged people to take risks and "jump the claim" that another legally owned; violence arose because claim holders and claim jumpers were equally protected under the law. This created chronic insecurity and litigation, not to mention conditions that encouraged miners to disrespect the

---

[36] *The Examiner*, "San Francisco Law and Order Forces Defeated," http://www.examiner.com/article/san-francisco-law-and-order-forces-defeated; "Vigilante Justice in the Gold Mines," http://www.examiner.com/article/vigilante-justice-the-mines; History Engine, "Crime and Instant Justice in Gold Rush California," http://historyengine.richmond.edu/episodes/view/5127; Calisphere, 1848-1856: Gold Rush Era, "Murder and Mayhem," http://www.calisphere.universityofcalifornia.edu/themed_collections/subtopic1a.html; SF Genealogy: San Francisco History, "The Annals of San Francisco (Part three: The Hounds), http://www.sfgenealogy.com/sf/history/hbann3-1.htm

claims of others. Miners thought the odds were in their favor and were rewarded at times. Given the chance to successfully steal the value of someone's land, which was limited and not always fixed until someone actually mined the property, it's no wonder that some disgruntled miners resorted to violence to right what they perceived as wrongs inflicted upon them.[37]

Chapter 7: Mining the Miners

The vigilance committees were established by the same men who had overseen a significant business revolution in mercantile products throughout California. While the Gold Rush will always conjure images of miners trying to find gold, most of the wealth was not in the hands of the miners in the fields but in the hands of the people trying to cater to the miners and sell them goods. Of course, as businesses generated more wealth in California, it produced an economic climate that jived with the risk-taking mentality of the gold rush. Entrepreneurs took bigger chances, and some produced their own type of booms. Kasler explained:

> "Some of the entrepreneurs started businesses that endured into the 20th century. Domenico Ghirardelli sold general merchandise to miners before devoting his full attention to chocolates. Korbel Champagne Cellars started as a maker of cigar boxes. John Studebaker made wheelbarrows for miners in Placerville, launching the company that eventually would make automobiles in Indiana. William Tecumseh Sherman co-owned a provisions shop in Coloma and was a banker in San Francisco before he became a legend of the Civil War. In Sacramento, the Rivett carpet company and Fuller-O'Brien paint company started out as one company, peddling glass and wall coverings. The four major titans of early California business -- Stanford, Crocker, Hopkins and Huntington -- made their money selling hardware in Sacramento before they moved to San Francisco and became railroad barons. There was tremendous land speculation; Front Street lots would change hands a dozen times a month."[38]

---

[37] Karen Clay, Gavin Wright, "Order Without Law? Property Rights During the California Gold Rush," Explorations in Economic History, http://www.stanford.edu/~write/papers/Order%20Without%20Law.pdf

[38] Gold Rush (Part Four: The Legacy), "Businesses, Banks Cashed in by 'Mining the Miners,'" http://www.calgoldrush.com/lb_sets/04business.html

Portsmouth Square in San Francisco during the Gold Rush

Meanwhile, miners attempted to sidestep the obstacles to instant wealth through their own associations and cooperatives. As the easy gold in rivers and streams "dried up," many had quickly come to realize that control over water would allow them to mine dryer terrain and climates. The companies that formed made miners employees in most cases, and some made a great deal of money. Control over water led to the innovation of hydraulic mining, which proved highly successful. Kasler writes, "As mining techniques became more sophisticated, so did these corporations. Early on, the miners used their own funds to start companies; they were the owners. By the mid-'50s there were companies with 50 to 100 miners -- many working as employees, for a day's wage -- backed by $200,000 or so in capital, much of it from New York or London."[39]

[39] Gold Rush (Part Four: The Legacy), "Businesses, Banks Cashed in by 'Mining the Miners,'" http://www.calgoldrush.com/lb_sets/04business.html
[39] Gold Rush (Part Four: The Legacy), "Businesses, Banks Cashed in by 'Mining the Miners,'" http://www.calgoldrush.com/lb_sets/04business.html

Miners using jets of water to excavate water from gravel beds

However, miners could not avoid the increasing connection between California's economy and the world. Finance capital did not need worker cooperatives; in fact, many businesses were better off with fewer workers, because improvements in mining technology required less miners to obtain the gold. Bigger machines extracted more of the surface earth, but the price of the mining technology grew enough to exclude more miners from the possibility of ever owning a company or even a stake in a company. Access to capital meant corporations could grow and expand the franchise of ownership to stockholders with access to capital, and of course, these stockholders could be businessmen completely removed from the region with no knowledge about how the mining actually worked.

To a large extent, San Francisco's rise to become one of the commercial centers of California occurred because of the presence of banking giants. The original service economy of the state worked on the exchange of gold dust, but this monetary system proved unstable and increasingly untenable in a world exchange economy. Banks rose up and private mints made coins, and the creation a U.S. Mint finally took place in 1854.

As it turned out, the rise of banks provoked a panic in 1855 that ruined the fortunes of miners with investments in banks. Bank runs took place and banks collapsed. One survivor of the bank failures was Wells Fargo; so many investors ended up in debt to Wells Fargo that the bank giant's biggest source of wealth came from the ownership of corporations.[40]

Over time, the rise of banks like Wells Fargo meant that corporations controlled the gold mines, and access to technology meant that the appearance of mining changed. The ability to accomplish the task of clearing away hundreds of thousands of years of sediment allowed hydraulic mining to take place; and the diversion of water, no small task even for a company, allowed dams to store water. The companies then used pumps and levers to apply extreme high pressure.[41]

RIVER OPERATIONS AT MURDERER'S BAR.

Illustration of miners excavating a dry bed after the water has been diverted

[40] Gold Rush (Part Four: The Legacy), "Businesses, Banks Cashed in by 'Mining the Miners,'" http://www.calgoldrush.com/lb_sets/04business.html; Wells Fargo, "Since 1852," https://www.wellsfargo.com/about/history/adventure/since_1852

[41] The Discovery of Gold in California (California Geological Survey - Gold Discovery), http://www.conservation.ca.gov/cgs/geologic_resources/gold/CA_GoldDiscovery_files/Pages/GoldDiscovery.aspx

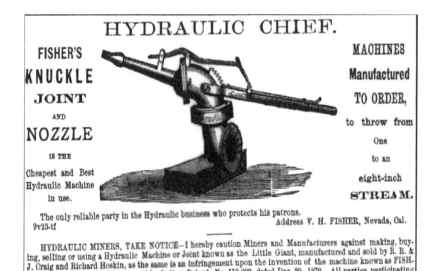

Advertisement for a hydraulic monitor

The corporations used mammoth monitors to get to the gold, some 14-16 feet long, blasting the hillsides and cratering mountains. 1.5 billion cubic yards of debris was washed down hillsides and into streams and valleys. Some river systems and wetlands were permanently buried under sand and rock. One observer commented on the damage.

"Tornado, flood, earthquake and volcano combined could hardly make greater havoc, spread wider ruin and wreck, than are to be seen everywhere in the track of the larger gold-washing operations. None of the interior streams of California, though naturally pure as crystal, escape the change to a thick yellow mud from this cause, early in their progress from the hills. The Sacramento River is worse than the Missouri. Many of the streams are turned out of their original channels, either directly for mining purposes, or in consequence of the great masses of soil and gravel that come down from the gold-washing above. Thousands of acres of fine land along their banks are ruined forever by the deposits of this character. A farmer may have his whole estate turned into a barren waste by a flood of sand and gravel from some hydraulic mining up stream; more, if a fine orchard or garden stands in the way of the working of a rich gulch or bank, orchard or garden must go. Then the tornout, dug- out, washed to pieces and then washed over side-hills, masses that have been or are being subjected to the hydraulics of the miners, are the very devil's chaos indeed. The country is full of them among the mining districts of the Sierra Nevada, and they are truly a terrible blot upon the face of Nature."[42]

Hydraulic mining

Though it's often forgotten, the major environmental impact of mining is what truly ended the California Gold Rush. At the peak of production, the environmental damage became so pronounced, with debris flooding and destroying farmland and preventing river traffic, that the farmers organized and demanded that legislators in Sacramento force the corporations to end the practice. In 1884, the California Supreme Court finally forced businesses to stop the destruction. This ruling ended the era of quick riches from gold mining, thus ending the boom period. More importantly, it was farming, not mining, that was king of California now.[43]

"The economic consequences and significance of the discovery of gold are equally great but harder to determine. Increased production in the United States, followed by increased foreign production resulting from the California gold rush, caused an increase of money in circulation. By 1865 in California alone $750,000,000 in gold had been mined, and this figure is considered a conservative estimate. In spite of the heavy

[42] Sierra College, "Monitors - Water Cannons of Hydraulic Mining," http://www.sierracollege.edu/ejournals/jsnhb/v2n1/monitors.html

[43] Gold Fever! "Giant Gold Machines - Hydraulic Mining," http://museumca.org/goldrush/fever19-hy.html

increase of circulating gold, the much-feared serious inflation, which was predicted by economists, failed to materialize. True, in California, at the source of gold and where commodities were scarce, initial inflation was tremendous; but world inflation as a result of the California gold rush and its successors, was slight."[44]

Chapter 8: The Legacy of the Gold Rush

The California Gold Rush will always evoke images of the common man panning for gold along the rivers and foothills of California, but of the 118 million ounces of gold that have been extracted from California since the discovery of gold there, most of it was accomplished through mining rocks and hard materials, the kinds of activities that lone miners couldn't accomplish by themselves. Some of the early miners unquestionably made fortunes worth millions of dollars in today's currency, but they were the exception to the rule. The wealthiest men in California during the Gold Rush were men like Samuel Brannan, who sold shovels and pickaxes to miners rather than attempt to strike gold himself. Levi Strauss made a fortune selling denim overalls to miners, and his name is still well-known in America as a jeans manufacturer.

Illustration of miners crushing quartz ore to find and extract the gold

In the immediate wake of the discovery of gold, California formed from the forces of the Gold Rush that intended to reward free enterprise and risk-taking individualism but also prevent undesirable competitors from challenging white Americans on the frontier. But the search for

---

[44] The Discovery of Gold in California (California Geological Survey - Gold Discovery), http://www.conservation.ca.gov/cgs/geologic_resources/gold/CA_GoldDiscovery_files/Pages/GoldDiscovery.aspx

riches in California, as well as other regions that helped support boomtowns throughout the frontier, also helped to bridge the new continental empire of the U.S. In addition to spurring westward expansion, wealth was created not just by mineral riches but by the creation of a vibrant economy that functioned in step with the rest of the global market. Americans appreciated that the achievement of instant wealth was possible, but they also witnessed the rapid growth of banks and corporations that created a state to support the monopolization of natural resources. The creation of California could not have happened without the arrival of gold, but it was not gold by itself that explained the passions of the "gold rush." Americans were committed to the ambitions of a nation to dominate the continent, and the Gold Rush was a manifestation of that Manifest Destiny.

Bibliography

Bancroft, Hubert Howe (1884–1890) History of California, vols. 18–24.

Brands, H. W. (2003). The age of gold: the California Gold Rush and the new American dream. New York: Anchor Books.

Heizer, Robert F. (1974). The destruction of California Indians. Lincoln and London: University of Nebraska Press.

Hill, Mary (1999). Gold: the California story. Berkeley and Los Angeles: University of California Press.

Holliday, J. S. (1999). Rush for riches: Gold fever and the making of California. Oakland, California, Berkeley and Los Angeles: Oakland Museum of California and University of California Press.

Johnson, Susan Lee (2001). Roaring Camp: the social world of the California Gold Rush. New York: W. W. Norton & Company.

Rawls, James, J.; Bean, Walton (2003). California: An interpretive history. New York: McGraw-Hill.

Starr, Kevin (1973). Americans and the California dream: 1850–1915. New York and Oxford: Oxford University Press.

Starr, Kevin and Richard J. Orsi (eds.) (2000). Rooted in barbarous soil: people, culture, and community in Gold Rush California. Berkeley and Los Angeles: University of California Press.

The Klondike Gold Rush

Chapter 1: Land of Gold

"The men and women who brave the perils of the wilderness to seek their fortunes in Alaska, go with a certainty that the treasure is there. It is a mere matter of finding it when once they have reached the fields. What is more the Land of Gold, as we may properly term Alaska, has proved and will prove to tourist and prospector as rich in delights and marvels as the land which has come down to us in legend. It seems to be a spot chosen by nature as a field of adventure. The person, therefore, who goes from the South to the Yukon Valley will be sure to find, even though disappointed in the quest for which primarily he went, enough of the beautiful and marvelous to pay him for his trip." - A.C. Harris, author of *Alaska and the Klondike Gold Mines* (1897)

Throughout the 19th century, the United States had a rich heritage of gold rushes, starting with the little-known 1828 Dahlonega Gold Rush in the Georgia town by the same name and then moving to the best known Gold Rush, which started in California in 1848. However, the most recent rush took place at the very end of the century in the much less forgiving climate of Yukon and Alaska, and while it did make a few men rich, it also served a much greater purpose by introducing Americans to what became the country's final frontier.

According to Robert C. Kirk, "While the credit for the discovery of gold in the Klondike is generally given to George Carmack, its actual discovery was due to the efforts of Robert Henderson, who entered the Yukon country in 1894. For several years Henderson prospected in the summer months on the tributaries of the Upper Yukon, and spent the winters hunting game near Sixty-Mile Post, a trading station located fifty miles above the present site of Dawson [City]. Among the rivers and creeks ascended by Henderson during 1895 was Indian River, which lies on one side of a low divide that separates it from the Klondike River. When Henderson entered Indian River it was late in the autumn, and there remained but a few weeks before the coming of the Arctic winter in which he could prospect for gold on the tributaries of this little river. But during this short time he succeeded in finding 'colors' of gold on what is now known as Australia Creek, and thus were sown the seeds that eventually ripened into the great discovery in one of the tributaries of the Klondike. Henderson remained on Australia Creek until October, living mainly by his rifle, until a shortage of flour and other staple provisions made it imperative for him to return to Sixty-Mile Post for a winter's outfit. Enthusiastic over the result of his find, he readily induced the store keeper at Sixty-Mile to advance sufficient flour to keep him alive until the following spring. He then descended the Yukon, and entered the mouth of Indian River, but, instead of continuing on to Australia Creek, turned into Quartz Creek, a tributary of Indian River, entering it on the north side. Henderson prospected alone on this river all the winter, living upon the supplies he had obtained at Sixty-Mile Post and the moose and caribou he killed with is rifle. It might here be noted that, had this wandering prospector crossed a single range of hills, he would have descended into El Dorado Creek, one of the world's richest placer streams, any claim of which would have sold twelve months afterwards for from forty to one hundred thousand pounds (or from one hundred thousand to half a million dollars)."

PA-016522

Henderson

Carmack

Skookum James, another discoverer of gold in the region

Although Henderson never made it to Eldorado Creek, thanks to his find and the way he bragged about it, thousands of others certainly would in the months to come. In the meantime, during the spring of 1896, "Henderson crossed the mountain divide separating the tributaries of Indian River from those of the Klondike, and wended his way to the bed of the stream that had never before felt the tread of a white man. This stream, which is a tributary of Hunker Creek, itself a tributary of the Klondike River, is now known as Gold Bottom. Among the surface sands and gravels of this creek Henderson discovered the tiny particles of placer gold known to the miners as ' colors,' and, after working about four weeks, returned to Sixty-Mile Post for supplies. While visiting the trading-post Henderson induced three men to go with him to Gold Bottom, where they subsequently recovered from the wash gravels in the creek bed one hundred and twenty-five pounds (or about seven hundred dollars) in 'dust' and nuggets."

Of course, this begs the question of how Carmack came to take credit for starting the gold rush. Kirk explained, "Henderson told Carmack that he had discovered gold on a creek on the Klondike side of the Indian River divide, and offered to take him to the spot so that he too might stake or 'peg out' a claim. … Carmack, realizing the fabulous richness of the find, hastily staked a discovery claim, which, according to the Canadian laws, is twice the size of an ordinary claim, and the two Indians [with him] were given the claims next adjoining on the upper and lower sides. Carmack, completely ignoring the fact that Henderson, who was primarily the author of his sudden wealth, was at work on an inferior claim across a range of hills, and was certainly entitled to one of the rich claims, left for Forty-Mile Post without sending Henderson any information of the strike. When he arrived at the Post Carmack told the miners there of the great strike; but, owing to the fact that he had previously claimed to have made discoveries, none of which had turned out successfully, the miners at first refused to listen to him. Presently, however, a stampede began for the new El Dorado, which was eventually to cause the abandonment and desertion of the mines and stores in and about Forty-Mile Post. A week later a second stampede came to the Klondike from the mines near Circle City, three hundred and eighty miles below Dawson; and when Henderson, who was still on Gold Bottom, heard of the discovery on Rabbit Creek, he found that all the claims for fourteen miles had been taken up, and that El Dorado and the other tributaries were each staked to an average distance of two miles. Henderson was broken-hearted when the full force of his misfortune dawned upon him and he found that it was impossible for him to get possession of a good claim."

In fact, it had long been known that there was gold in faraway Alaska, but even in the late 19th century, problems with transportation and communication made it too difficult to get to for all but the most seasoned explorers. Nonetheless, the prospect of finding gold, especially within the context of the financial crisis of 1893, was enough to compel a large number of men, and even some women, to take their chances. Inevitably, these newcomers were a tremendous source of irritation for the more established miners, as one of them, Francois Mercier, admitted, "What makes my blood run faster in my veins is to think that I have walked all over that gold and that now others are digging it. It prevents me from sleeping at night."

Even with the interest brought about by the announcement of gold, the Klondike Gold Rush would be different in that it started slow and then gained momentum. As A.C. Harris noted in 1897, "In the gold mining regions of Alaska there were, in 1893, not more than about 300 miners all told. This number was doubled practically the following year. Owing to the glowing reports of successful operators, the number of miners attracted by 1895 was 3000. Probably twice that number of miners and prospectors invaded the country in 1896. In 1897 came this furor that caused the Klondike district to rank with the great historical gold fields of the world. This year witnessed the greatest influx of people into the territory on record, and there was every prospect that the year following would see the number quadrupled, possible many times over."

Chapter 2: A Seal of Ice

"Not until July 14th, 1897, was the news received. There arrived at San Francisco an ocean steamer. She came from the north, and from a region hitherto locked against human interest by a seal of ice. Few had ever gone there, and of that few some were returning now, and under circumstances such as attract public attention when most other attractions fail. They were almost literally laden with gold. And from them a name was heard almost for the first time. The region they had left is called The Klondike. They were a strange company. No ship since the old Californian days had unloaded so motley a cargo. It was midsummer, but they had left the

Klondike at the earliest possible moment. Their belongings were peculiar. What baggage they carried was tied up in old blankets and pieces of canvas with ropes. Hundreds of people who did not know them, and had never heard before of the new land of gold, suddenly attracted, watched them as they came ashore." - James Steele, author of *The Klondike* (1897)

While much of the gold mined out of the area could be reached through traditional methods such as panning or working with a pickaxe, the real money lay in the deep veins, and those who knew this tried to warn the others. Professor S. F. Emmons of the United States Geological Survey was quoted in 1897 as having said, "The real mass of golden wealth in Alaska remains as yet untouched. It lies in the virgin rocks, from which the particles found in the river gravels, now being washed by the Klondike miners have been torn by the erosion of streams. These particles, being heavy, have been deposited by the streams, which carried the lighter matter onward to the ocean, thus forming, but gradual accumulation, a sort of auriferous concentrate. Many of the bits, especially in certain localities, are big enough to be called nuggets. In spots the gravels are so rich that, as we have all heard, many ounces of the yellow metal are obtained from the washing of a single panful. That is what is making the people so wild — the prospect of picking money out of the dirt by the handful literally."

Even without the ability for most to mine deeply into the earth, there was still money to be made, and within weeks of the first major strike, R.E. Preston of the United States Mint noted, "That gold exists in large quantities in the newly discovered Klondike district is sufficiently proven by the large amount recently brought out by the steamship companies and miners returning to the States who went up into the district within the last eight months. So far $1,500,000 in gold from the Klondike district has been deposited at the mints and assay offices of the United States, and from information now at hand there are substantial reasons for believing from $3,000,000 to $4,000,000 additional will be brought out by the steamers and returning miners sailing from St. Michael's the last of September or early October next. One of the steamship companies states that it expects to bring out about $2,000,000 on its steamer sailing from St. Michael's on September 30th, and has asked the government to have a revenue cutter to act as a convoy through the Behring Sea. In view of the facts above stated I am justified in estimating that the Klondike district will augment the world's gold supply in 1897 nearly $6,000,000."

Preston also added, "The gold product of Alaska thus far has been remarkable rather for its regularity than its amount, and is therefore more favorable to the permanency of development of the mineral resources than if it were subject to violent fluctuation. Nature seems to have sprinkled Alaska and all Asiatic Russia with gold. The latter region sends annually over $25,000,000 to the mint at St. Petersburg. The production of gold there is such that the annual output of the Russian Empire would, it is claimed, exceed $50,000,000 were it not for the obstacles put in the way of human industry by an inclement climate and an inhospitable soil."

It is difficult to give a hard and fast date for the beginning of the Klondike Gold Rush, but it took a big leap forward in the fall of 1896 when the "Chechockoes," out of Portland, Oregon, began to report their big strikes. In 1897, Captain William Kidston observed, "These men, are every one what the Yukoners call 'Chechockoes ' or newcomers, and up to last winter they had nothing. Today you see them wealthy and happy. Why, on the fifteen days trip from St. Michael's I never spent a pleasanter time in my life. These fortunate people felt so happy that anything would suffice for them, and I could not help contrasting them with the crowd of gold hunters I took with me on the last trip up. They were grumblers, without a cent in the world, and nothing on the boat was good enough for them. Some of these successful miners do not even own claims. They have been working for other men for $15 a day, and thus have accumulated small fortunes. Their average on this boat is not less than $10,000 to the man, and the very smallest sack is $3000. It is held by C. A. Branan, of Seattle, a happy young fellow just eighteen years old. There is no country on earth like the Yukon."

One thing that made the Klondike Gold Rush possible was the relative ease with which people could now get to Alaska, especially from the West Coast. Steamships had been perfected by this time, and many plied the waters back and forth up the West Coast and Canada. One, the *Willamette*, left for Alaska on August 7, 1896, and according to one account, "The most excited and largest crowd of people that has ever gathered on the ocean docks in this city, on any occasion, gathered to-day to see the steamer Willamette off for Alaska. Four hundred people boarded the vessel here, and their friends and relatives and thousands of sight-seers gathered to see the start. The passengers came from all parts of the State and a sprinkling from all over the United States. The baggage was carried mostly on horseback, only a few mules being used. The pack trains marched through the city in droves, and Grand Army men said it reminded them of war times. All sorts of outfits for making money were taken aboard, from a baker to gambling tables. Nearly every person aboard has a list of from six to three dozen persons who had been promised letters. Fathers parted from families and young men from their sweethearts at the docks. Not a few of the men have pledged their families and friends that they will not return from the Eldorado of the North, until they have amassed a fortune, if it takes ten years to accomplish it. Aboard this vessel, Tacoma sent forward its first installment of physicians and surgeons to the Klondike. The doctors will dig for nuggets, if they cannot get patients."

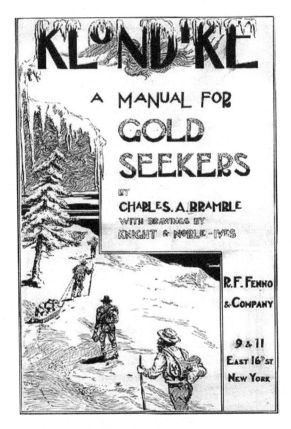

An 1897 manual for miners

Another person present at the dock that day but sailing on a different ship wrote, "The *Alki* started for Alaska this afternoon with 125 passengers, 800 sheep and 50 horses. Crazed with the gold fever and the hope of reaching Klondike quickly, the passengers bade good-bye to thousands on shore, who were crazed because they could not go. Food, comfort, sleep were ignored in the fierce desire to get to the gold fields. Those who could not go to Alaska stayed on the dock all day, shaking hands with those who were going, and gazing with eyes of chagrin and envy on the lucky ones as the steamer started for the North. There was grim pathos in the scene on the dock while the gold hunters were waiting for permission to go on board. Some were taking passage who would surely never leave Alaska alive. They had heard stories of the returned miners, that health was an absolute requisite in the terrible climate of the Klondike district. They smiled and knew better. One man said he was suffering from lung trouble, but that he might as well die making a fortune as to remain on the shores of Puget Sound and die in poverty. Not an inch of room was left on the *Alki*. It was tested to its utmost capacity. Excited men, drunk with visions of fortunes, were huddled among the sheep, horses and baggage. Space was valuable, and a cattle pen had been constructed on the main deck, which had hitherto been reserved for passengers. The sheep were put on board only after the crowd had been driven back from the steamer. On the main deck the horses and sheep will stay until the journey by water is ended. When port is reached the pen will be reduced to its original state and the lumber put to new use."

A picture of the SS *Excelsior* leaving San Francisco for the Klondike in July 1897

The steamship *Islander* leaving Vancouver for the region in 1897

Chapter 3: A Fortune in Gold

"On Wednesday, July 14th, 1897, the little steamer Excelsior arrived in the harbor of San Francisco with forty miners on board, each one of whom had brought with him from the icebound interior of Alaska a fortune in gold. From that day may be said to date the Klondike gold craze which already rivals in extent the three other great gold crazes of the century, California in 1849, Australia in 1851 and South Africa in 1890. Already the amount known to have been brought back by the returning miners exceeds $4,000,000, and nearly $3,000,000 more is said to be on the way. It is estimated by some experts that before the full returns come in it will be found the total output of the Alaskan mines has been $8,000,000. California yielded $60,000,000 five years after Marshall's discovery, and all from place diggings, as are the diggings in the Klondike region; but the facilities for mining in California, with its salubrious climate, its comparative nearness to civilization, its all-year-round conveniences, were infinitely superior to the facilities in the Yukon Basin." - L.A. Coolidge, author of *Klondike and the Yukon Country* (1897)

A map of routes taken to the Klondike

Another aspect that set the Klondike Gold Rush apart from some of the previous strikes was that there was an early interest on the part of big business in getting in on the action. People on the West Coast were not the only ones to be affected by the Klondike Strike because back east, investors on Wall Street were anxious to learn how they could get a piece of the action. In July 1897, one paper reported, "Wall Street has been seized by a genuine ' '49 ' gold fever as a result of the discoveries in the Klondike. Men who have mined and made money; men who have mined and lost money; men who have always thought they might speculate a little in mining, and men who have had a complete abhorrence of mining; — all seem to be affected the same way. More than half a dozen banking concerns, and as many individuals in Wall Street, whose Standing in the financial world is the very best, have actually turned away from $5000 to $125,000 each which clients and customers wished to invest, under their guidance and supervision in the great gold fields of Alaska. ... The prejudice against mining is waning. Only recently bankers who dabbled in mines were looked upon with about as much suspicion by their customers and the money world as a bank clerk or cashier who regularly played fare, roulette and the races. Rut that is wearing off and the best concerns are beginning to mine in one way or another."

Those who wanted to make money without enduring the hardships of mining could do so by loaning money to those who were going out to mine in return for a percentage of whatever they found. Needless to say, this was a tricky business, as one could never be sure what would happen, but many remained optimistic. The same article reported, "Seven men living near Trenton, N. J., 'grub-staked' by business men of Trenton and merchants of Philadelphia, started in April for the Alaska gold fields. W. J. Hibbert headed the expedition. He writes that they have laid claim to eighty miles of dredger land, and have received a grant of twenty-one placer claims, which will be added to the dredger lands. He says that the ground is rich, and within a mile and a half of their claim a man by the name of Lereno, after working five days, found, on clearing up, that he was worth $40,000 in gold. Another story told by Hibbert in his letter is that another miner, after two months' work, was $ 150,000 to the good."

Daniel Guggenheim, part of the M. Guggenheim & Sons firm, noted, "For some time my firm has had expert mining engineers at work in Alaska, and their reports leave no doubt that the Yukon gold fields will prove the richest in the world. My opinion is that as soon as the country has been opened up and shipping facilities furnished the output of gold will be simply enormous. As the production of gold increases silver will be enhanced in value. This I regard as certain."

Not everyone was as optimistic. For example, one Chicago investor noted, "If I were to give you the details of some of the schemes that have been submitted to me recently for making money in the Klondike, you would think some insane asylum had been thrown open, and the inmates turned loose. Some of the ideas are not bad in themselves, but are impracticable owing to the conditions of the country. Others are simply the rankest form of lunacy, while others yet are downright swindles. People who would not even think of suggesting a fraud in connection with ordinary business have no hesitation in boosting up a fraud in a mining boom. As a rule, however, the irresponsible schemers are merely wild-eyed cranks, who have an honest confidence in their own plans."

One of the main things that concerned those who had been in Alaska for a while at the start of the rush was the way in which men abandoned the steadily working mines to go after a dream of bigger strikes. In 1897, Dr. C. F. Dickenson of Kodiak Island said, "When I left Kodiak, two weeks ago, the people were leaving all that section of country and flocking in the direction of Klondike. In a way, the situation is appalling, for many of the industries are left practically without the means of operation. Mines that were paying handsomely at Cook's Inlet have been deserted. In my opinion there are just as good placer diggings to be found at Cook's Inlet as in the Klondike region. There is not a foot of ground in all that country that does not contain gold in more or less appreciable quantities. There is room there for thousands of men, and there is certainly no better place in the world for a poor man."

Miners in a shaft in 1898

Pictures of mining operations circa 1899

While most people were most interested in getting rich, authority figures around the Alaskan tundra and the surrounding areas were also concerned about what kind of impact the rush would have on their region. 50 years earlier, the California Gold Rush proved to be the very making of the state; even after the '49ers were done, the state grew into one of the most populous and prosperous ones in the country. As a result, Alaskan officials wondered if the same thing would happen to their territory.

A couple of police officers with dogs

The federal government and local officials weren't the only ones concerned. In a report filed with the Canadian government in November 1896, William Ogilvie, a land surveyor, claimed, "A branch of Bonanza, named Eldorado, has prospected magnificently, and another branch, named Tilly Creek, has prospected well; in all there are some four or five branches to Bonanza which have given good prospects. There are about 170 claims staked on the main creek, and the branches are good for about as many more, aggregating say 350 claims, which will require over 1000 men to work properly. A few miles further up Bear Creek enters Thron-Diuck (Klondike), and it has been prospected and located on. About twelve miles above the mouth Gold-bottom Creek joins Thron-Diuck, and on it and a branch named Hunter Creek very rich ground 'has been found. One man showed me $22.75 he took out in a few hours on Hunker Creek with a gold pan, prospecting his claim on the surface, taking a handful here and there as fancy suggested. On Gold-bottom Creek and branches there will probably be 200 or 300 claims. The Indians have reported another creek much farther up, which they call 'Too Much Gold Creek,' on which the gold is so plentiful that as the miners say in joke you have to mix gravel with it to sluice it. From all this we may, I think, infer that we have here a district which will give 1000 claims of 500 feet in length each. Now, 1000 such claims will require at least 3000 men to work them properly, and, as wages for working in the mines are from $8 to $10 a day., without board, we have every reason to assume that this part of our territory will in a year or two contain 10,000 souls at least. And this is not all, for a large creek, called Indian Greek, joins the Yukon about midway between Thron-Diuck and Stewart Rivers, and all along this creek good pay dirt has been found. AH that has stood in the way of working it heretofore has been the scarcity of provisions and the difficulty of getting them up there. Indian Creek is quite a large stream, and it is probable it will yield five or six hundred claims."

No matter what his opinion was at that moment, Ogilvie knew that the situation was in a constant state of flux. He filed another report the following December, "Since my last the prospects on Bonanza Creek and tributaries are increasing in richness and extent, until now it is certain that millions will be taken out of the district in the next few years. On some of the claims prospected the pay dirt is of great extent and very rich. One man told me yesterday that he washed a single pan of dirt on one of the claims on the Bonanza and found $14 in it. Of course, that may be an exceptionally rich pan, but $5 to $7 per pan is the average on that claim, it is reported, with five feet of pay dirt and the width yet undetermined, but it is known to be thirty feet even at that. Figure the result at nine to ten pans to the cubic foot, and five hundred feet long; nearly $4,000,000 at $5 per pan — one fourth of this would be enormous. Another claim has been prospected to such an extent that it is known there is about five feet pay dirt averaging $2 per pan and width not less than thirty feet. Enough prospecting has been done to show that there are at least fifteen miles of this extraordinary richness, and the indications are that we will have three or four times that extent, if not all equal to the above at least very rich."

Chapter 4: Veins of White Quartz

"It may be said that the rocks of the gold belt of Alaska consist largely of sedimentary beds older than the Carboniferous period; that these beds have undergone extensive alteration, and have been elevated into mountain ranges and cut through by a variety of igneous rocks. Throughout these altered rocks there are found veins of quartz often carrying pyrite and gold. ... Many of the veins have been cut, sheared and torn into fragments by the force that has transformed the sedimentary rocks into crystalline schist; but there are others, containing gold, silver and copper, that have not been very much disturbed or broken. These more continuous ore-bearing zones have not the character of ordinary quartz veins, although they contain much silica. ... Concerning the veins of white quartz first mentioned, it is certain that most of them which contain gold carry it only in small quantity, and yet some few are known to be very rich in places, and it is extremely probable that there are many in which the whole of the ore is of comparatively high grade." - Edward Spurr, author of *Through the Yukon Gold Diggings*

By 1897, the question on everyone's minds was how long the gold rush would last. While many people rushed north in fear that it would be gone before they got there, many of those who had studied the situation believed that there was enough gold in Alaska and the Yukon to keep people digging for a long time. John V. Mackay, who had made his fortune in California in 1849, predicted, "I have no reason to doubt [the reports coming out of Alaska]. 'I have had great confidence in the mining possibilities in British Columbia and Alaska — have always believed that those frozen, almost inaccessible regions contain heavy deposits of precious metals. Some enormous 'finds' of gold have undoubtedly been made there, and yet we know little or nothing of the possibilities of the country. Think of Williams' Creek, for instance, in the Caribou region in British Columbia. As long ago as 1860 something like fifty millions of gold were taken out. It was placer mining there, just the same as the Klondike. Capital will always go where there is a chance for legitimate investment, and transportation facilities will increase as rapidly as the travelers. I see in it, something like the excitement of the early fifties over the gold discoveries of the Pacific coast region. The reports of rich individual finds are likely to continue, and the arrival of every ship loaded with fortunate gold hunters will stimulate the imagination, hopes and desires of the would-be gold hunters. We hear nothing of the failures. One man who is lucky is more talked about than a thousand who fail."

A more intellectual authority who approached the issue from a purely scientific point of view agreed. Dr. W.H. Dall, then at the Smithsonian Institution back in Washington, saw both the potential and the challenges facing the miners: "The gold-bearing belt of Northwestern America, contains all the gold fields extending into British Columbia and what is known as the Northwest Territories and Alaska. The Yukon really runs along in that belt for 500 or 600 miles. The bed of the main river is in the valley. The yellow metal is not found in paying quantities in the main river, but in the small streams which cut through the mountains on either side. Mud and mineral matter are carried into the main river, while the gold is left on the rough bottom of these side streams. In most cases the gold lies at the bottom of thick gravel deposits. The gold is covered with frozen gravel in the winter. During the summer until the snow is all melted, the surface is covered with muddy torrents. When summer is over and the springs begin to freeze, the streams dry up. At the approach of winter, in order to get at the gold the miners find it necessary to dig into the gravel formation."

Another question on everyone's mind was whether there was a hidden mother lode with riches beyond all imagination, and if so, what its location would be. George Frederick Wright, a geology professor at Oberlin College, mused, "Placer mines originate in the disintegration of gold-bearing quartz veins, or mass like that at Juneau. Under subaerial agencies these become dissolved. Then the glaciers transport the material as far as they go, when the floods of water carry it on still further. Gold, being heavier than the other materials associated with it, lodges in the crevices or in the rough places at the bottom of the streams. So to speak, nature has stamped and 'panned' the gravel first and prepared the way for man to finish the work. The amount of gold found in the placer mines is evidence not so much, perhaps, of a very rich vein as of the disintegration of a very large vein. What the prospectors have found points to more. The unexplored region is immense. The mountains to the south are young, having been elevated very much since the climax of the glacial period. With these discoveries and the success in introducing reindeer. Alaska bids fair to support a population eventually of several millions."

Mining engineer William Van Slooten agreed that there were plenty of indications of more gold "upstream:" "No such specifically large amounts of gold were taken out by individuals during any similar period of California gold hunting. Two months of work in the water has realized more than any six months heretofore known in the history of gold mining. We had long been aware that there was gold in the Yukon basin, but the total output for the last ten years before the Klondike developments amounted to not more than a million dollars' worth at the utmost. Now, within two months, five millions have been taken out of the Klondike regions. It took the first eight months of work in California to pan out that amount under infinitely more favorable conditions of climate and weather. That is a straw worth noting."

Congress had actually sent a team of researchers to Alaska in June 1896 to get an idea of how much gold might be there, and in reporting the expedition's findings, Spurr told Congress, "No quartz or vein mining of any kind has yet been attempted in the Yukon district, mainly on account of the difficulty with which supplies, machinery and labor can be obtained; yet it is certain that there is a vast quantity of gold in these rocks, much of which could be profitably extracted under favorable conditions. The general character of the rocks and of the ore deposits is extremely like that of the gold-bearing formations along the southern coast of Alaska, in which the Treadwell and other mines are situated, and it is probable that the richness of the Yukon rocks is approximately equal to that of the coast belt. It may be added that the resources of the coast belt have been only partially explored. ... Since the formation of the veins and other deposits of the rocks of the gold belt an enormous length of time has elapsed. During that time the forces of erosion have stripped off the overlying rocks and exposed the metalliferous veins at the surface for long periods, and the rocks of the gold belt, with the veins which they include, have crumbled and been carried away by the streams, to be deposited in widely different places as gravels, or sands, or muds. As gold is the heaviest of all materials found in rock, it is concentrated in detritus which has been worked over by stream action; and the richness of the placers depends upon the available gold supply, the amount of available detritus, and the character of the streams which carry this detritus away."

As for the everyday miners, Spurr made the following observations: "In Alaska the streams have been carrying away the gold from the metalliferous belt for a very long period, so that particles of the precious metal are found in nearly all parts of the Territory. It is only in the immediate vicinity of the gold-bearing belt, however, that the particles of gold are large and plentiful enough to repay working, under present conditions. Where a stream heads in the gold belt, the richest diggings are likely to be near its extreme upper part. In this upper part the current is so swift that the lighter material and the finer gold are carried away, leaving in many places a rich deposit of coarse gold overlain by coarse gravel, the pebbles being so large as to hinder rapid transportation by water. It is under such conditions that the diggings which are now being worked are found, with some unimportant exceptions. The rich gulches of the Forty Mile district and of the Birch Creek district, as well as other fields of less importance, all head in the gold-bearing formation. A short distance below the heads of these gulches the stream valley broadens and the gravels contain finer gold more widely distributed. Along certain parts of the stream this finer gold is concentrated by favorable currents and is often profitably washed, this kind of deposit coming under the head of "bar diggings." The gold in these more extensive gravels is often present in sufficient quantity to encourage the hope of successful extraction at some future time, when the work can be done more cheaply and with suitable machinery. The extent of these gravels which are of possible value is very great. As the field of observation is extended farther and farther from the gold-bearing belt, the gold occurs in finer and finer condition, until it is found only in extremely small flakes, so light that they can be carried long distances by the current. It may be stated, therefore, as a general rule, that the profitable gravels are found in the vicinity of the gold bearing rock."

Spurr concluded his report with an observation about those currently engaged in mining: "There were probably 2000 miners in the Yukon district during the past season, the larger number of whom were actually engaged in washing gold. Probably 1500 of them were working in American territory, although the migration from one district to another is so rapid that one year the larger part of the population may be in American territory and the next year in British. As a rule, however, the miners prefer the American side, on account of the difference in mining laws. These miners, with few exceptions, were engaged in gulch digging. The high price of provisions and other necessaries raises the price of ordinary labor in the mines to $10 per day, and therefore no mine which pays less than this to each man working can be even temporarily handled. Yet in spite of these difficulties there were probably taken out of the Yukon district the past season, mostly from American territory, approximately $1,000,000 worth of gold."

An 1898 picture of prospectors buying mining licenses in British Columbia

Chapter 5: The Tenderfoot and the Old-Timer

People en route to the Klondike

"Those who join the stampede to a new goldfield may generally be divided into two classes, the tenderfoot and the old-timer; otherwise, the novice and the experienced prospector. The novice joins the stampede because he catches the 'fever'—dreams dreams. The old-timer goes because the diggings he had last worked in proved of little good. Were the sea-dogs of old-- Drake, Raleigh, or Frobisher--born into the world to-day, their spirit would surely have impelled them to the mining camp, to seek fortune in the mountain fastnesses, and to wager years of effort on the chance of wresting from Nature her treasure stores. On the steamship _Aleutian_, as she lay in the dock at Vancouver, British Columbia, one day in the March of 1898, there were many tenderfeet and a few old-timers. Amongst the experienced was John Berwick. About him surged the steamship's host of passengers, waving their arms, and yelling answers to the cheer that went up from the great crowd upon the dock-side. He and his fellows were bound for the Klondike goldfields. Before them lay adventures, toil, and danger; the adventurous will ever draw the tributes of goodwill from the multitude staying at home." - William Henry Pope Jarvis, the author of *The Great Gold Rush: A Tale of the Klondike*

No matter where he came from, once a prospector arrived in Alaska, the first goal was to try to find a good place to dig. If the prospector found somewhere that was as yet unclaimed, he would "stake his claim." According to Kirk, who spent a year in the Klondike, "The miners stake the claims in the following manner — presuming, of course, that a 'discovery 'has been made upon a hitherto un-located creek. The first 'stampeders ' to arrive drive their stakes, or 'pegs, ' immediately on the upper or lower boundary line of discovery claim, as they may select, and then pace off 500 feet, where they erect two other stakes, one on each side of the creek, against the hill. Upon all of these stakes, which, by law, must be four feet high, and have four-inch faces, the miner writes the day and date, and ' I claim 500 feet up stream [or downstream, as the case may be] for mining purposes. 'He then signs his name and writes the number of his 'free miner's license, 'which was previously issued to him by the Government for the sum of two guineas (or ten dollars). The next man arriving stakes off the next 500 feet, and so on, until the whole creek has been staked, when the belated arrivals usually try their luck on one of the different tributaries to this new creek. Within three days from the time of staking, the miner goes before the Gold Commissioner in Dawson, and, after swearing that he has staked the claim in accordance with the law, he receives a certificate, costing three guineas (fifteen dollars), which entitles him to the exclusive right to mine for gold upon this particular claim for one year, at the termination of which he ^has the privilege of renewal. He has no surface rights to the ground, but is permitted to cut cabin logs for a house and wood for use in his mine."

Picture of a wagon stuck in mud in Dawson City in 1898

Miners in Dawson City in 1899

The Dawson City Post Office in 1899

Once the prospector had the legal rights to the land, he or she could begin to mine for gold. According to Kirk, how the prospectors accomplished this depended on where they were mining. "The methods employed in recovering the gold from the alluvial gravels of these creeks are peculiar to the gold-fields of the Klondike. To understand this system it must first be known that the gold-bearing gravels were deposited at a very early age, and that, in consequence of the enormous amount of debris torn away from the hill-sides by erosion and deposited in the beds of the older and larger creeks below, these gravels are buried to a depth varying from twelve to thirty-five feet. The intense cold of the long winters, and the consequent perpetual frost, has put an additional lock upon these vast treasuries of wealth by freezing the gravels solidly together. The debris covering the gravels consists of layers of sand and 'muck' — a black substance, consisting of sand, decomposed vegetable matter, &c, — all of which is cemented together by frost. In order to reach the gold-bearing gravel the miners first sink a shaft through the muck, which is found to be extremely brittle in its frozen state, the small pieces that fly in all directions under the blows of the pick being so thin and sharp that they pierce the skin and flesh with which they come in contact. Some miners prefer to build fires in the muck and shovel it to the surface in a thawed state, but others believe that it can be pierced more rapidly by ' picking ' it up frozen. When the shaft reaches a depth at which it becomes impossible for the miner to shovel the dirt to the surface a simple rope windlass is erected, and the dirt is hoisted in a bucket by a second miner, who remains on top."

This description explains why so many of the most successful miners worked in pairs or groups. Kirk continued, "When the muck is pierced and frozen gravel is encountered it becomes impossible to proceed further without fires. Consequently, both dry and green wood is sledded to the mine by dog-teams, and when this is split to the required fineness it is lowered into the shaft. The fire is built by first placing a layer of finely-split dry pine covered by heavier pieces of very dry wood. A second layer of green wood is then placed on this, the object being to produce a fire that will burn longest and 'hold the heat.' When all is ready the fire is lighted with a candle, the latter being used because experiment has shown that the temperature of the split wood, corresponding with the extremely low temperature of the surrounding atmosphere, must be brought to a certain degree of heat before it will ignite, and that matches are practically useless for lighting in the ordinary degree of cold. When the fire is once started it burns with exceptional vigor and fierceness, because the hot air, rising so rapidly in the cold, produces an intense draft. Gradually, then, the miner picks his way downward through the frozen gravel until he reaches bed-rock, testing his prospects each night in his cabin, where he thaws the pans of gravel over the fire. If the pay-gravel is rich enough and the layer is thick enough to warrant further development, he begins drifting — that is, he tunnels along the line of bed-rock, carefully building his fires so that only the gravel in the ' face ' (or end) of the tunnel is thawed, and not that of the roof (or 'over-hang'), which would entail an extra amount of unnecessary shoveling. No timbering is necessary to keep the 'over-hang' from falling, because the frost holds the gravel in place, and there is absolutely no danger from caving. At night the miner builds his fire, which burns fiercely until early morning, when it gradually dies out, and the perpetual draft caused by the heated gravel clears the shaft of smoke."

Kirk described what came after the fire melted enough of the permafrost to allow the miner to extract earth: "The miner then descends the shaft, and, after shoveling back the 'waste ' gravel that contains no gold, he proceeds to send up the pay-dirt in the wind-lass bucket. His working partner, who remains on the surface, empties the gravel and returns the bucket for another load. In this way two men, working together, will place from one hundred to one hundred and eighty buckets of pay-dirt on the surface each day, the buckets holding about seven 'pans' apiece. Every night the miner from the shaft washes a prospect pan or two, to tell if the pay-dirt is improving or losing in value, and on the following day builds his fires in the direction of the best prospects. These 'pannings' are usually thrown into a discarded baking-powder can, or similar receptacle, and usually provide pocket money for an occasional trip to Dawson. Ordinarily, these 'pannings' amount to from one hundred to one thousand dollars (or from twenty to two hundred pounds), and even more, during the mining season. The length of time during which the mines may be worked by the drifting system just described seldom exceeds five months, and more often it will scarcely last four months. The surface water usually makes it impossible to begin operations before November, and by the middle of March the weather has so moderated that the smoke and gases from the wood fires refuse to leave the shafts, making it impossible for the miner to descend. Several deaths have already occurred in the Klondike mines from suffocation by gas and smoke."

While many nostalgically imagine miners looking down at buckets of newly gathered earth and seeing a shiny golden nugget, it rarely happened that way. Instead, the dirt had to be processed to be made valuable. Kirk explained, "It is seldom that the miner in the shaft, except on the richest claims, or the windlass man above, ever finds a nugget while the gravel is being excavated; these are always revealed by water in the prospect pan. Frequently small particles of gold can be seen in the gravel dumps when the gravel is first thrown from the bucket, but the moment it freezes they become practically invisible."

After months of hauling dirt from the ground, the excitement came in the spring when it was time to "wash" it. Again, this usually required teamwork, as Kirk noted: "The miners remain at work until the spring thaw brings the season's operations to a close. The warm sun gradually melts the great heaps of frozen gravel that have been thrown up on the surface, and by the time the miners have set the sluice boxes the 'pay- dirt' is ready to be 'shoveled in.' The process of sluicing is practically the same as in other countries. A dam is built across the creek-bed at a convenient distance above the gravel heaps, and when the water rises to the required height it is led in wooden boxes or troughs to the claim. A 'puddling-box,' which is usually sixteen feet long and about three feet six inches wide at the widest place, is fitted with heavy pole 'riffles,' and in this stands a miner in rubber-boots, whose duty it is to throw out the larger rocks, after they are thoroughly washed, so that they will not clog the smaller boxes below. The gravel is usually shoveled into the small boxes above the 'puddling-box.' These are also fitted with pole 'riffles,' but their pitch is such that the debris is washed almost instantly into the 'puddling-box.' Below this last box are from two to six small boxes fitted with riffles, and having a fall of from five to ten inches to the box length (twelve feet). After two or three days' run, the boxes are carefully cleaned of rocks and gravel, the riffles are lifted and the gold and black sand, of the latter of which there is a great abundance in the Klondike, are carefully separated, by water, in the ' puddling-box.' Finally, the gold is placed in a miner's pan and carefully dried over a fire, when the line grey sand which refused to be separated from the gold by water is easily blown away, so that nothing remains but the pure gold. The 'dust' and nuggets are then weighed by ounces, and when this number has been multiplied by the value of an ounce, the result of the 'shift' is definitely known."

Over time, the miners developed a system to help each other and divide both the work and the profits. Kirk later recalled, "Both the creek and bench claims are frequently worked by the ' lay,' or lease system. This implies that the miners contract with the owner of a claim to work a section of, perhaps, fifty feet of the claim, and agree to give the owner a percentage (usually 50 per cent.) of the output. The miners then supply everything needed to recover the gold, and the claim-holder has practically no responsibilities. The owners of the richest claims, however, prefer to work their ground by day -wages, because the actual cost of recovery is much less than 50 per cent. The gold recovered from the claims on El Dorado Creek is of a dark, brassy colour, and assays about…about fifteen dollars to the ounce. The gold from the other creeks averages much better, the best quality being found on Hunker and Dominion Creeks. Bonanza gold is bright in colour, and assays about…sixteen dollars to the ounce."

Prospectors working near the Yukon River

Chapter 6: Inexperienced Miners

Skagway at the beginning of the White Pass Trail in 1897

WINTER TRAIL UP THE WHITE PASS MAR 29-99.

Miners on White Pass Trail in March 1899

"Every new enterprise is marked by innumerable mistakes. All inexperienced miners load themselves with things they afterwards throw away. For such a journey the most primitive necessities of life only can be carried, and for such a country as Alaska all we mean by the word "clothing" in civilized life must be cast aside. Underwear is made of heavy blanket flannel. Coarse, strong trousers, the heaviest and most durable made, must be worn. Foot-wear must be coarse, heavy and strong. The coat should be a pea jacket. A "slicker," by which is meant a water- proof coat, should be carried. The fur-lined sleeping bag of the arctic regions is a necessity. A few tin pans and cups, and a frying-pan and coffee-pot, constitute the cooking vessels. A pick and a long-handled spade are the chief needed tools. To go loaded with fire-arms is foolish, though one rifle to a party, and a good revolver per man, is not superfluous." - James Steele

In time, it became clear that while gold was the usual motivating factor for people coming to the region, they came to the Klondike for all sorts of reasons. For some, the Klondike Gold Rush was a second chance at glory, an opportunity to return one more time to the excitement and adventure of their youth. E. J. Baldwin, a West Coast millionaire who had made his fortune during the big California Gold Rush of 1849, could have increased his fortune from the safety of his own home by investing in a miner or two, but he decided to go to Alaska himself. He explained his thinking in 1897: "I will not stop at Klondike, but will push right into the mountains, where I am sure there must be rich quartz ledges. Ample machinery will be shipped to Dawson or elsewhere, if I succeed in locating a paying claim. I think the big fortunes will be made in the quartz districts and not in the placers, which will be sure to give out if so many thousands of people will persist in rushing into the country. I am going next spring, and expect to take twenty-five or thirty husky young men with me who can work and endure the hardships. I am seventy-one years old, but still feel strong enough to do a little prospecting. It is also my intention to take a lot of machinery along for lode mining. My notion of the situation there is that the placer mining they are carrying on is an indication that there is gold in large quantities back in the mountains. I shall hunt out these deposits, and, equipped with modern machinery, will do a regular mining business. I am convinced the gold is there; consequently, I will be taking no long-risk chances."

Speaking from his earlier experience as a miner, Baldwin suggested that each man heading to Alaska outfit himself with the following items for the first month:

"chocolate, 7 ½ pounds, or tea, 3 ¾ pounds;

rolled oats, 7 ¼ pounds

navy beans, 22 ½ pounds

bacon, 37 ½ pounds

flour, 30 pounds

salt, 3 ¾ pounds

pickles, 60 cents' worth

cayenne pepper, ¼ pound for eighteen months

four cakes dry yeast"

What set Baldwin apart from many fellow miners was the fact that he had real life experience in the ups and downs of gold mining. For most, it was a new adventure. The failures quietly licked their wounds and the successful ones boasted of their newfound wealth, adding fuel to the fire. One of the success stories was G. H. Cole, who wrote to his wife, "This is a wonderful country. There is enough gold here to load a steamboat. Lots of men have made all they want since last fall, and gone out. There is hardly a day but there is from one to half a dozen come from the mines with all the gold they can carry. One man had so much he had to get several men to help him carry it out. He gave the mine to a friend to do what he wanted with it. He was a Seattle man. Some of the men who have been out to the mines say there is more gold here than they ever saw in their lives, and some of the old miners, who have been in most all the mining countries in the world, say it beats anything they ever saw. Around some of the camps they have it piled up like farmers have their wheat, and in other camps they have all their cooking utensils full of gold and standing in corners as if it were dirt. Some are taking out S100,000 a day. Old miners say there has been enough gold located to dig up for the next twenty years."

For most, the hope of striking it big was seen as a chance, often a last chance, to capture life's ever-elusive riches. After striking it big, Clarence Berry admitted, "Yes, I am a rich man, but I don't realize it. My wife and little ones will, though. I took out my gold last winter in box lengths twelve by fifteen, and in one length I found the sum of S10,000. The second largest nugget ever found in Alaska was taken out of my claim. It weighed thirteen ounces and is worth $5230. Why, I have known men to takeout $1000 from a drift claim, and some have taken out several thousand. This gold was found in pockets, and it is not an ordinary thing to make such marvelous finds. Yes, there is plenty more of gold there. I expect to take many more thousands from my claim; others on this boat expect to do the same. Those who have good claims will undoubtedly be millionaires in a few years. The gold will not give out for a long time. There is room for more miners in Alaska, but they must be strong men, must have money, and should know about mining. The hardships are many. Some will fail to make fortunes, where a few are successful. A man may have to prospect for many years before he finds a good claim. That means that he needs money and strength to help him along ; but if he sticks to it he will come out all right."

Prospectors on the frozen Crater Lake in 1898

Pictures of prospectors at the beginning of Chilkoot Trail

Many of those coming to Alaska arrived from other countries, like Dougal M'Arthur, who came to America as a young man: "I left the good Old Country when a mere boy, determined, if possible, to carve out a fortune for myself. Coming to America I drifted from place to place with varying success and finally, six years ago, determined to try my luck in Alaska. It was hard working at first, but I soon got used to it, and I determined to stay there until I struck something that would pay me for my trouble. At Forty-Mile camp I made some money and then I drifted over to Circle City. There I did not do so well, but I kept pegging away, believing like Micawber, that something would turn up after a bit. Well, last of all came the news of a tremendously rich strike on the Klondike. We — that is, my partner, Neal McArthur and myself — pulled up stakes and started for the new discovery. Neal went ahead and was fortunate in locating a good claim. My part of the work consisted in hauling our provisions and camping outfit over the snow and ice to the new location. I was compelled to make two trips, and it was the hardest work I ever did in my life. I reached Dawson City finally just two days before Christmas. Neal had prospected the claim and found it rich beyond our fondest anticipations. Before we could begin work there was an offer to buy it and we sold out for $50,000. It was a lucky turn of the wheel of fortune for us. Without practically a stroke we cleaned up $25,000 apiece. Now we are going home to see our people. My own folks have not heard from me in a long time, and maybe they think I am dead. It will be a joyful home-coming for all."

Fred Price was another one who won the Klondike lottery: "I was located on the Bonanza with Harry McCullough, my partner. I brought down $5000 in gold dust and made $20,000, which is invested in more ground. There were good stakes on the boat coming down — from $5000 to $40,000 among the boys. I refused $25,000 for my interest before I left. My partner remains, and I shall return in the spring after seeing my family in Seattle. I was in the mines for two years. One can't realize the wealth of that creek. There are four miles of claims on the Eldorado, and the poorest is worth $50,000. The Bonanza claims run for ten miles, and range from $5000 to $90,000."

Of course, not everyone who was mining during the gold rush was able to stay with it for a long time. An older man named August Galbraith conceded, "The development of Alaska has only just begun. If I were not an old man, I would have remained where I was. There is no doubt in my mind that all of the country for hundreds of miles around Dawson is rich in gold. It is the best place that I know of for a poor man to go. If a man has $300 when he starts, well and good, for it may be useful if he should not be fortunate the first season."

One article written at the time described J.O. Hestwood as "a typical returned Argonaut," and he went on to write of his adventures after he left his Seattle home to try his luck in the gold fields of Alaska. "With hundreds I rushed to the new fields. After a few days I became disgusted and started to leave the country. I had gone only a short distance down the river when my boat got stuck in the ice and I was forced to foot it back to Dawson City. Well, it was Providence that did that. I purchased claim No. 60, below Discovery claim, and it proved one of the richest pieces of ground in the district. My claim will average 16 or 17 dollars to the pan, and in addition to what I have already taken out, there is at least $50,000 in … it. Last season I worked thirty men, and I intend to employ more next year."

Finally, there is the story of L.B. Rhoads, who reported, "I am located on Claim 21, above the discovery on Bonanza Creek. I did exceedingly well up there. I was among the fortunate ones, as I cleared about $40,000, but brought only $5000 with me. I was the first man to get to bedrock gravel and to discover that it was lined with gold dust and nuggets. The rock was seamed and cut in V-shaped streaks, caused, it is supposed, by glacial action. In those seams I found a clay which was exceedingly rich. There was a stratum of pay gravel four feet thick upon the rock, which was lined with gold, particularly in these channels or streaks. The rock was about sixteen feet from the surface."

The Yukon River, Klondike City (foreground) and Dawson City (background right)

Dead horses on White Pass Trail

Chapter 7: Exceptionally Rich

Prospectors on the Dalton Trail

"As far as is known at the present time there are six creeks in this region that are exceptionally rich. On the Klondike side of these summits there are El Dorado, Bonanza, Hunker, and Bear, flowing north; while on the Indian River side of the water-shed are Dominion and Sulphur Creeks. … El Dorado, which is undoubtedly the richest creek in the district, is a tributary of Bonanza, joining it at a point about half a mile from discovery claim. It is somewhat broader near the mouth than Bonanza at the point of confluence, and this fact, considered an objectionable feature by the miners, caused it to be left to the last before anyone could be induced to stake, or "peg-out," a claim. Adams Creek, a tributary of Bonanza about a mile below El Dorado, was staked for three miles before a peg was planted on El Dorado Creek, and the fact that Adams Creek is practically devoid of gold, and El Dorado fabulously rich, illustrates the fallacy of miners trying to estimate the value, or worthlessness, of a creek merely by the surface indications and the general appearance of the surrounding country."

While gold mining occasionally resulted in quick money, it almost never resulted in easy money. Alexander Orr made $12,000 but he also complained, "In winter the weather is extremely cold at Dawson, and it is necessary that one be warmly clad. The thermometer often goes sixty or seventy degrees below zero. Ordinary woolen clothes would afford little protection. Furs are used exclusively for clothing. Dawson is not like most of the large mining camps. It is not a 'tough' town. Murders are almost unknown. A great deal of gambling is done in the town, but serious quarrels are an exception. Stud poker is the usual game. They play $1 ante and oftentimes $200 or $500 on the third card."

Thomas Cook agreed: "It's a good country, but if there is a rush, there is going to be a great deal of suffering. Over 2000 men are there at present, and 2000 more will be in before the snow falls. I advise people to take provisions enough for eight months at least. If they have that, it is all right. The country is not exaggerated at all. The mines at Dawson are more extensive and beyond anything I ever saw."

One of the most telling stories was that of Allan McLeod, who came to Alaska from Perth, Scotland. While he made it back home with nearly $100,000 in gold, his adventure nearly cost him his health: "I went to Alaska early last summer, with a crowd of miners who came up the Sound from San Francisco. I was out of money and work, or I doubt whether I would have accepted the offer they made me to go along as cook. We reached Cook's Inlet June 20th, and things looked so discouraging we went back to Juneau. There we bought supplies and started for Dawson City, 750 miles away. We camped there, and I did the cooking for the boys. They did very well, but the gold fever took them farther east, and I remained to cook for another gang of miners. I made good wages, and finally had enough to start a restaurant. In two weeks I sold the place $5000, and went placer mining with…a partner. We had good luck from the start, and I would have remained but for a severe attack of inflammatory rheumatism. It would have killed me but for the nursing of my partner. He carried me most of the way to Juneau, where I got passage on a fishing schooner to 'Frisco. I am satisfied with what I've got in money, and hope to get rid of my rheumatism before long. Great fortunes are being found by many men, and no one knows the extent of the gold fields that are constantly developing."

Another man, M.S. Norcross, admitted that there was more than one way for someone to make his fortune: "I was sick and couldn't work, so I cooked for Mr. McNamee. Still I had a claim on the Bonanza, but didn't know what was in it because I couldn't work it. I sold out last spring for $10,000, and was satisfied to get a chance to return to my home in Los Angeles."

John Marks summed up his experience and that of most of the miners when he said, "I brought back $11,500 in gold dust with me, but I had to work for every bit of it. There is plenty of gold in Alaska — more, I believe, than the most sanguine imagine — but it cannot be obtained without great effort and endurance." In a similar vein, Talbot Fox offered this warning to those considering joining the rush: "I and my partner went into the district in 1895 and secured two claims. We sold one for $45,000. I brought 300 ounces, which netted 5000. Everybody is at Dawson for the present. The district is apt to be overrun. I wouldn't advise anyone to go there this fall, for people are liable to go hungry before spring. About 800 went over the summit from Juneau, 600 miles, so there may not be food enough for all."

Lieutenant John Bryan was on the Revenue Cutter Rush and stationed with the United States Navy in Unalaska, Alaska when he wrote home to his family in Lexington, Kentucky, "You dig no deeper than fifteen feet into the river bed when you strike a strata of pure gold nuggets among the stones. There are eighty claims already taken, each 5,000 feet long and the width of the river bed. The great obstacle in reaching the gold field is the uncomfortable mode of travel. Steamers go no further than the mouth of the Yukon, and you have to walk the 1000 miles or pay the extra agent fare asked by the company, which runs a small boat up the river and finally lands you near the gold fields. All who are fortunate enough to reach the country are certain to find employment, even if they do not strike a claim, which at present they could avoid only by not looking for it. The poorest miners will pay fifteen dollars a day for help op their claims, but it will cost five dollars per day to live unless you take your provisions with you." Still, he admitted that if he hadn't already made a commitment to Uncle Sam, he would happily try his hand at mining.

If he had any plans to join the gold rush after he finished his tour of duty, Bryan likely opted to go to Nome rather than the Klondike, because the rush ended almost as quickly as it began in 1899. The previous year, the newspapers that had once found the Klondike Gold Rush so fascinating lost interest in the story and moved on to other topics. By this time, most of those who had "gold fever" had already made it to Dawson City or some other place, only to find it overcrowded and already mined. Then, in 1899, gold was discovered to the west in Nome, Alaska, so most of those who were still interested in mining abandoned the Klondike region for new opportunities there. By 1900, Dawson City was nearly a ghost town.

Picture of a ship leaving the Klondike for Nome

A picture of prospectors selling goods before leaving the area

Even though the rush was over, there was still gold in the region, and companies began to be formed to use heavy duty mining equipment. For the next several years, they dug out much of what the small-scale miners had missed, but even these efforts were mostly over by the end of 1902.

For a while, it seemed that the great Klondike Gold Rush would fade into the dustbin of history, especially since it paled in comparison to the California Gold Rush. However, in 1960, the popular American country music singer Johnny Horton came out with a song paying tribute to those early miners. Called "North, to Alaska," the song soon made it to the top of many American music charts.

"North to Alaska, You go north, the rush is on
North to Alaska, I go North, the rush is on

Big Sam left Seattle in the year of ninety-two
With George Pratt, his partner and brother, Billy, too
They crossed the Yukon River, And found the Bonanza Gold

Below that old white mountain, Just a little south-east of Nome

Sam crossed the majestic mountains (mush)
To the valleys far below (mush)
He talked to his team of huskies (mush)
As he mushed on through the snow (mush)
With the northern lights a-runnin' wild (mush)
In the land of the midnight sun (mush)
Yes, Sam McCord was a mighty man (mush)
In the year of nineteen-one (mush)

Where the river is windin' Big nuggets they're findin'
North to Alaska They go North, the rush is on"

Even to this day, there are still some gold seekers who continue to search for the elusive mother lode in Alaska's frozen tundra. However, at least some of them have learned that the real money lies in the gold mine of reality television; there are currently several television shows built around the cultural descendants of those first men who went "north to Alaska."

Bibliography

Adney, Tappan (1994). *The Klondike Stampede*. Vancouver, Canada: University of British Columbia Press.

Berton, Pierre (2001). *Klondike: The Last Great Gold Rush 1896–1899*. Toronto, Canada: Anchor Canada.

Bramble, Charles A. (1897). *Klondike: A Manual For Goldseekers*. New York, US: R. F. Fenno.

Fetherling, George (1997). *The Gold Crusades: A Social History of Gold Rushes, 1849–1929*. Toronto, Canada: University of Toronto Press. ISBN 978-0-8020-8046-2.

Mole, Rich (2009). *Gold Fever: Incredible Tales of the Klondike Gold Rush*. Surrey, Canada: Heritage House.

The Chicago Record (1897). *Klondike. The Chicago Record's Book for Gold Seekers.* Chicago, US: Chicago Records Co.

Made in the USA
Coppell, TX
08 December 2019